JIGSAW, SOME PIECES MISSING

JIGSAW

SOME PIECES
MISSING

memories of
childhood and youth

LOUISA FOULKE NEWLIN

FOUR WINDS
— PRESS —

ISBN (paperback): 978-1-94042-318-0

Book design: Domini Dragoone
Cover photo: Dmitry Demidov/Pexels
Author photo: Nick Newlin
Family photos from the author's personal collection

Published by
Four Winds Press
San Francisco, CA

For my beloved granddaughters,
Elizabeth Kim Newlin Carney,
Louise Ho Newlin,
and Nicole Ho Newlin

CONTENTS

PART II: YOUTH

Dear son Bill, Nick, Eliza,
Louise, Nicole, and Elizabeth,

The world has changed enormously since I was a child. Anyone over eighty can say this, and could in any century, but that does not make it less true. When I first became aware of my surroundings at about the age of about five, there was of course no internet, cell phones, or social media. Independent bookstores abounded. Television was probably being developed, but we had no TV at home until I was fourteen. Civilian air travel, even after the War (which was World War II) was very limited; I did not go on an airplane until I was sixteen.

The recollections that follow are not in strict chronological order. Some are portraits of key people in my early life, others describe a school or a particular period of time. I cannot say that everything here is "true," only that I have set down events and impressions as I remember them. I hope that some of these memoirs will entertain you and evoke what looks, at this distance, like a blessed and more innocent era.

With great love,
Mom/Granny

PART I

CHILDHOOD

…light winged Dryad of the trees,

In some melodious plot

Of beechen green, and shadows numberless,

Singest of summer in full-throated ease.

—JOHN KEATS,
Ode to a Nightingale

BEECHEN GREEN

I t was my father, an English major at Princeton, who came up with the name for our house. It had originally been a stable, now converted into a spacious fieldstone residence at the bottom of a long, steep driveway which was hazardous in icy winters. The mailing address, for years, was just "End of West Chestnut Hill Avenue, Chestnut Hill, Pennsylvania." No house number, no zip code. It was surrounded by four acres of land on the edge of the wooded Wissahickon Park, where we used to take family walks on Sunday afternoons, accompanied by a bumptious, brown and white springer spaniel named Bobby.

No chestnut trees in the park, though, or anywhere else in Chestnut Hill; they had been killed off by a blight in the 1920s.

My earliest memories are of this house. I think I remember my new baby brother Walter being presented to me by my mother when I was three, and watching his diapering intently. His anatomical difference was christened his "doodad," by Yan, the British nanny who joined our family when I was three months old. She shared this name with Miss Mac, a fellow nanny, who used to say to Walter when the two went walking together, pushing prams, "How's your doodad?" Miss Mac had to stop when he was old enough to know what it meant, and Yan dropped it too.

I don't remember feeling jealous of Walter's presence, though I doubtless reacted negatively to being pushed out of the limelight. We shared a big bedroom, called "the nursery" by Yan. I had been moved into a big-girl bed a year earlier, and the crib I had occupied was moved back in for Walter. There was a child's wooden table, painted blue, with an attached chair, in which I sat for meals and for practicing writing the letters Yan taught me. I remember the thrill of realizing that, by putting different letters in front of "at," I could make different words: Cat! Sat! Mat! Rat! When I outgrew the table, Walter used it, and later on, my second brother, Billy. It is still in the family, passed on to a great-niece who is too big for it now. It's waiting for the first great-grandchild.

Another memory is of being scolded for cutting all the hair off a doll as I sat on my bed. I expected it to grow back, as my own did, and had trouble explaining this when I was reprimanded. And still another: tearing around the room with Walter in a wild improvised dance to a record of Grieg's "In the Hall of the Mountain King," from the Peer Gynt suite, turning the volume up and knocking over lamps and books in our mad career. Yan confiscated the record. "Too stimulating," she said.

There was a bathroom connecting the nursery with Yan's room. My parents' bedroom, which had a fireplace, was off the hall on the opposite side. They slept in twin beds, which were fashionable for a couple of decades—I am not sure why. I think it had to do with liberating women from the constant demands of the conjugal bed in an era without reliable birth control. Their windows overlooked the garden, and ours overlooked the driveway and the path into the Wissahickon. Yan's room connected to a back hall off which were two smaller rooms and a bathroom; these were occupied by a cook, Irish Annie Dealy, and a series of very young Irish maids, most called Nora. (Annie, my father liked to recall later, stirred cake batter with her hand, a detail that has stuck with me. Annie said this made the cakes lighter.) As children usually do, I accepted the circumstances of my life unquestioningly, including the presence of Yan, Annie and a succession of Noras and Bridgets who cleaned and waited at table.

Other early memories: leaning out the nursery window and seeing Tony, the Italian gardener, planting a tree in the earth outside the dining room. "What is that?" I asked. "Itsa pinka dogwood," he answered cheerfully. There was another, taller tree right outside that window, on one of whose branches a robin built a nest. Three blue eggs appeared. I was fascinated. "Don't keep staring at them, Lou," Yan warned. "You'll scare the mother bird away." I couldn't stop, and the bird did abandon her nest, and I wept. "No use crying over spilt milk," said Yan, and I puzzled over what spilt milk had to do with the robin's departure.

We moved from Beechen Green to Cape May, New Jersey, in 1941, when I was five. My father had joined the Navy and had been assigned to the base in Cape May, where the Coast Guard station had been transformed into a Naval base, "for the duration." For a long time, I thought the word "duration" meant "war."

After the War, my father was honorably discharged from the Navy, and we moved back to Beechen Green, where I lived until I was married. My parents lived there until 1979, when they moved into a smaller and more manageable house, also in Chestnut Hill, but conveniently closer to Germantown Avenue, the main street, without Beechen Green's long, steep driveway, and with a first-floor bedroom. My mother christened it "Rose Grange." By this time, I was forty and the mother of teenagers. Bill and I visited Rose Grange often, but despite the comforting presence of the familiar furniture and painting, it never really felt like home.

IT WASN'T UNTIL after the war, when the family was reunited and I was nine, that I was welcome at dinner, which was supposed to be a "civilized occasion." "Civilization" was an important concept, since, according to my parents, it had almost disappeared from the earth, and only the Allies, led by Roosevelt and Winston Churchill, had saved it from our enemies, the Axis. Perhaps my parents thought that naming the house after a British Romantic poet encouraged Civilization.

Until I was promoted, I had dinners in the nursery with Walter and Billy, supervised by Yan, who did her best to teach us table manners. My brothers were eventually promoted too, at progressively younger ages, to my annoyance; Walter achieved the dining room table at eight, and Billy at six, when Yan was no longer with us.

Dinner took place in the gracefully proportioned dining room with its banks of casement windows on two sides, through which one could see rhododendrons, frozen and drooping in winter, flowering pink and white in spring. There were two birdcages on stands, one for a canary, the other for a pair of parakeets. The room must look very different now: I hear the new owners turned it into a family room for watching television. We sat around the polished mahogany table, which had been brought back on "the boat" from a trip to England my father took with his widowed mother before the War; my parents were engaged, and the purpose of the trip was to buy furniture for their new household. Except on Thursdays and Sunday evenings, when my mother cooked, dinner was prepared by Mary Ann Sweeney (Annie Dealy had retired) and served by a Nora. We were expected to eat everything on our plates—starving children in Europe were regularly invoked. If we didn't, we risked getting what was left back at the next meal. Exceptions were made for foods our parents determined were "acquired tastes," like lamb kidneys. Walter was a picky eater, and sometimes was presented at lunch with the oatmeal he had rejected at breakfast. (It's a wonder he didn't develop an eating disorder.)

There were rituals. My mother made the salad dressing at the table, mixing the oil and vinegar from the antique silver cruet stand she prized, with a big wooden salad spoon. There were ground rules. No talking with your mouth full, no interrupting, no tattling. There were occasional abrupt departures from Civilization, like the time I laughed with my mouth full of milk, which I sprayed all over the table, and was sent to my room in disgrace. We were expected to carry on conversations, not just about school or piano lessons with the dreaded Miss Gillette, but about books, history, and selected current events. Not, however the atrocities of the War now coming to light at the Nuremburg Trials, from which my parents and Yan tried to shield us. Because of its disturbing photographs, *Life* magazine was not permitted in the house. Since it was forbidden fruit, I sought it out eagerly at the houses of friends or at the dentist's office, and looked, appalled, at pictures of returning concentration camp survivors, the horror intensified by seeing them secretly.

We discussed safe books, like *Ivanhoe* and *Quentin Durward* (I was deeply into the Middle Ages for several years), and I remember insisting that Sir Walter Scott had written *Men of Iron.* My parents said No, it was Howard Pyle. I ran upstairs to check the book—we were allowed to disappear briefly to fact-check . They were correct. I was crestfallen. "Why do you always have to be *right?*" my mother asked in exasperation, not for the first time. We did not discuss movies much until I was around twelve and allowed to see pre-approved ones on Saturday afternoons at the Hill Theater, long since defunct, with my friends. Until I was fourteen, we didn't discuss television, because we didn't have one. Walter wore my parents down with a drumbeat of talk about being the Only One In The Class whose family did not have a TV, and they finally broke down and bought one, after I had gone to boarding school, where there was no television. I didn't develop a taste for television until, much later, advertisement-free programs began to appear.

PHILADELPHIA SUMMERS ARE hot and humid, and there was no air conditioning then, not in private houses, not even in the bank where my father worked. On "real stinkers," the entire staff, officers included, were sent home early. My mother did her best to make the house seem cooler. The wool dining room rug was rolled up, removed to be cleaned and stored, and replaced by a woven mat from the Philippines. Cream-colored linen slipcovers went on to the living room sofa and upholstered chairs. Summer meant jellied consommé garnished with lemon and parsley, cold chicken with home-made mayonnaise, and iced tea with mint from the garden. We children were allowed to run through the sprinkler in our bathing suits, an unalloyed joy.

In the attic, there was an exhaust fan, which was supposed to draw heat up from the house through strategically placed registers and expel it though vents in the roof. When you flipped the switch in the back hall, it triggered off an ominous hum, which quickly warmed up to a gratifyingly loud roar. Walter and I, nine and six, used to torment our hapless three-year-old younger brother, Billy. We told him there were grizzly bears up in the attic, and we would lure him into the back hall, turn on the switch, and dissolved into hysterical laughter when he heard the roaring and ran howling for our mother or Yan. Why on earth were we so mean to our good-natured younger brother? Mercifully, he says he doesn't remember any of it. He does remember the sign my father had made, as a joke, saying "Beware of the Grizzlies," which he stuck into the ground at the bottom of our driveway. This alarmed many who drove down it, including the milkman, and had to be removed.

When we were older, we were sometimes taken to swim at the Penllyn Club, about five miles away, outside the city limits. Although it was in the country, it bore no resemblance to a "country club"; it was a deliberately simple place, in keeping with the tastes of its largely Quaker membership. No golf course, perhaps one tennis court. The centerpiece was a breathtakingly cold, clear, spring-fed swimming pool.. This was pre-Salk vaccine, and fear of polio was widespread—we were kept firmly away from all heated, crowded pools. My parents had faith in the Penllyn pool, "since the water keeps moving," they said. The heart-stopping shock of plunging into that pool on a hot day, the tingly feeling when I emerged, are sensations which, eighty-plus years later, I recall with immense pleasure. I still like swimming in cold water.

I SEE MY father arriving from the train station at the end of a hot day, dripping, his seersucker jacket over his arm, his tie loosened. After changing into a blue polo shirt and slacks, he and my mother sit on the flagstone terrace on the edge of the garden, drinking Tom Collinses. She's wearing a fresh cotton dress, yellow. Both are enjoying the dappled late afternoon light while we children race around the lawn in bare feet.

The War is really over. While it went on, my parents have often said, they thought they would never again be able to live the way they had. They are in their very early thirties, glowing with love and with gratitude at being reunited. During this green and golden time, our family is living in a post-Armageddon Eden. Or so it seems now.

chapter two

ONE OF MY MOTHERS

Y an-Yan, soon just "Yan," arrived in my life when I was three months old. Her real name was Gladys Smith. She was, as Grandpa, my grandfather Wood, used to say, "a sticker." (He adored her, and called her "Smitty," which no one else would have dared.) She didn't leave until my youngest brother, Billy, went to school, when I was eleven. She was English, and although she became an American citizen and lived in this country for most of her life, she never really stopped being English. One of her favorite stories was about going for a citizenship interview, during World War II. The interviewer asked her if she would be willing, if necessary, to take up arms against Great Britain. "Certainly not!" she said indignantly and marched out of the interview. Later, when the War was over, she did go through the process to citizenship. Whether she was again asked the offending question, I don't know.

The colonies of the British Empire, and the British Isles themselves, were colored pink on the globe on a stand in our library. "The sun never sets on the British Empire," Yan would say with satisfaction, pointing out the pink parts, and then sometimes, for emphasis, she'd sing a line or two from "Rule, Brittania."

Rule, Brittania! Brittania rule the waves!
Britons never, never, never shall be slaves!

Until I went to college, I felt as loyal to England as to the United States and was almost as proud as Yan was that so much of the globe was pink. This was well before the days when the whole idea of Empire fell into permanent disrepute and pink on the globe gave way to a rainbow of independent colors.

Her nickname may have started as a corruption of "Nanny," although Yan was very clear that she had been trained in England as a Nursery Governess, capable of giving lessons in a schoolroom, and therefore a notch up from a nanny, who was technically a nurse for babies and children under four. A nanny eats in the kitchen, or the servants' dining room, with the rest of the domestic staff;

a nursery governess gives lessons in the schoolroom, eats with her charges, either in the nursery or, when the children are old enough, at the table in the dining room with the rest of the family. World War I had blurred some of the distinctions of the traditional British servant hierarchy, and in America they had not existed in the first place, so Yan was willing, and more than able, to do work theoretically beneath that of "governess," like laundry and "light cooking" for us children. She taught us all to read and write a little before we went to school, a task more in keeping with her skills, which must have given her satisfaction.

What brought her to the new world in the first place? The Depression and a lack of opportunity in England? A spirit of adventure? She never said. Her first job in America was with the Glendennings in Philadelphia. They had one child, Betsy, and were divorced shortly after Yan came to work for them. Yan became Lily Glendenning's trusted ally, and they remained friends until Lily's death from cancer, long after Yan had left the household. She kept in touch with Betsy all her life, as well as with us and with the Prizer children, Johnny and Carla, who became "her children" after she had left us. When Yan died in her seventies, I was able to locate Betsy and the Prizers to tell them, and all wrote warm letters about her to be read at the service.

My mother was twenty when I was born in April 1936, and my father was twenty-three. Young parents, by most measures. In July, my father found himself between jobs. He had left the tile factory in whose offices he had been working in Philadelphia and had been hired by a New York investment firm but was not due to report there until the fall. He was invited by Tom Clark, one of his college roommates, to be an usher in the wedding to an Englishwoman, in England, in August. Muzzie, his mother, who was always one for seizing the day where travel was concerned, encouraged him and Mum to go, and said I could stay with her. She would hire a nurse. My parents decided to accept the offer, to go to the wedding, and to make a six-week trip out of the occasion. Crossing the Atlantic in 1936 took more than a week on an ocean liner. Who knew when they would be able to take so much time off again? As things turned out, they did not get back to Europe for sixteen years. They were always glad they had gone while they could.

During the Depression, the vast majority of people could not consider the luxuries of European travel, or six weeks off, or baby nurses. Mum and Dad could, thanks to my mother's frugal Quaker family, the Woods, who had invested prudently; and even more thanks to my father's maternal great-grandfather, a minor robber-baron who had built up a considerable pile in coal. Muzzie hired Yan to look after me, supposedly just for the summer. She came superbly recommended by Lily Glendenning, eager to place Yan well, as she couldn't continue to employ her—her income had shrunk drastically after her divorce. Muzzie became so attached to Yan, and so sure that she was a peerless nurse, that when my parents returned, she offered to pay half Yan's considerable salary for the following year. It was an offer they couldn't refuse.

When I became a mother myself, in the intensely child-centered fifties, I often wondered, a little resentfully, how my parents could have left me for six weeks when I was so new. But they themselves had had nannies when little, and the whole notion of having someone else care for your child seemed perfectly okay to them and to their own parents. Until I was around six, it seemed entirely normal to have Yan and Mum both. Perhaps the moment when I questioned my divided mothering for the first time was when, one day on the beach at Mantoloking, a boy my own age said to me, "One of your mothers is calling you."

When they returned from Europe, my parents moved with Yan and me to New York City, to an apartment that made my parents claustrophobic, especially my mother. They missed the quiet, green serenity of the Philadelphia suburbs and quickly began plotting their escape. They retreated to Philadelphia after ten months. My father went to work for the Provident Trust Company, and he and my mother rented "Beechen Green" in Chestnut Hill, the house described in the previous chapter that they later bought and where I lived until I married, apart from two indelible years in Cape May. As a college student stimulated by the flash and bustle of New York during my visits there, I asked my mother why on earth they had ever moved back to stodgy Philadelphia. "Because we thought no one in all of New York City cared one little bit about us!" she cried, an answer I understood only partially then.

My parents told Yan that, even though she was wonderful, they could not afford to keep her once they moved back to Philadelphia. My father later liked to tell the story of how Yan then went to the Russian Tea Room to have her fortune told. She asked what her new position would be, and the fortune-teller said she didn't see any new position in the crystal ball, which puzzled Yan. When she got back to the apartment, my father told her that Muzzie had once more intervened with a generous offer of financial help and that they hoped she would stay on. According to my father, Muzzie had said, "You can't buy love!" Quite true, but it has always struck me that in this case, after all, money had made the difference between love staying and love packing its bags. This I never said to my father—he liked his story too much.

So Yan came with us to Chestnut Hill, and then to Cape May when I was six and Walter was three. In Cape May, a Navy town during the war years, we had no maid and only intermittent cooks who came by the day. Yan rose to the occasion, as my parents said, and she and Mum managed between them, joking about their joint change in status. We all moved back to Chestnut Hill, after V-J day, when I was nine, and by that time, we had Billy, born in 1942, and were a complete family.

My daughter Eliza gave me recently a framed picture of Yan holding my baby self, which confirmed my memories of her appearance. She was slim and kind-looking, with reddish "permed" hair in a forties style with poodle bangs. She was attractive if not beautiful, and had "beaux," as my parents called them, who took her to the movies on Thursdays and Sunday afternoons, her days out. She was somewhere in her late thirties, older than our pretty mother by perhaps eight years. She never would tell me her age. My parents knew it but kept her secret. She was devoted to us children, and we to her; she was, like all good teachers, firm but fair. We knew she loved us, even though she prevented us from doing things she thought might spoil us, like going to the movies or eating ice cream in the middle of the afternoon. Whining for toys or treats was nipped in the bud. She would say, "You can't have everything you want," a dictum whose sad truth I have often been obliged to acknowledge. In addition to believing implicitly in the British Empire, she believed in a stiff upper lip; in Winston Churchill; in tea made with loose leaves in a pre-warmed teapot; in a well-regulated life including an eight-thirty bedtime, even in summer; in fresh air and in long daily walks no matter what the weather; in saying you were sorry right away when you had been rude or mean; in being polite even when politeness was not merited; in writing prompt thank-you notes; in Pond's Cold Cream; and in the benefits of stewed prunes.

We were not allowed, ever, to feel sorry for ourselves. When I would complain about having to polish my shoes or pick up my room, she would say, "You have a hard life" or "Stuff and nonsense!" If I whimpered over a skinned knee, she would say, "You'll die after it." It was years before I understood the meaning—that the knee would get well long before I died. If I came down to breakfast scowling, Yan would say cheerfully, "Here comes Gertie Grump," which made me laugh and restored my good humor.

Yan loved a good laugh and she loved to sing. Sometimes she embarrassed me by singing too loudly in church, especially at Easter. She belted out with gusto "Jesus Christ is risen today, A-a-a-a-a-leluia!" and "There is a green hill far away, outside a city wall/Where our dear Lord was crucified/Who died to save us all." At home, she sang songs like "I love sixpence, jolly, jolly sixpence" and World War I songs like "Wish me luck, as you wave me goodbye!" and "Pack up your troubles in your old kit bag," made famous as a marching song in World War I:

Pack up your troubles in your old kit bag
And smile, smile, smile.
While you've a Lucifer to light your fag,
Smile boys, that's the style!
What's the use of worrying?
It never was worthwhile—
So pack up your troubles in your old kit bag
And smile, smile, smile.

She told us that every day when she was at school during that war, the war of *her* childhood, a classmate would be weeping over the death of a father or an uncle. (Her own father, mercifully, was too old for the army.) When I went to England for the first time, when I was sixteen, I saw everywhere long lists of young men killed in that war—on monuments, on the wall of Eton School, on the walls of country churches—and thought of Yan and her grieving friends, and of a whole nation in mourning.

My mother told me when I was an adult, that she had been conflicted about sharing us with Yan, who was more experienced in child care and whose authority she did not want to question. Mum felt insecure about her own capabilities and, like my father, was convinced that we children had a better chance at being tidy, well-behaved, and above all *unspoilt* children if cared for by Yan. "Spoiled" was for Yan a condition to be avoided above all. My father clearly thought that having Yan allowed my mother to be a more attentive, devoted, and attractive wife. "Your mother wouldn't look so young and pretty if we hadn't had Yan," he was fond of saying. Then they would gaze lovingly at each other across the table.

It was Yan who introduced me to Charlotte Bronte's *Jane Eyre*, when I was ten. Having heard that it was about a governess, she had checked it out from the Chestnut Hill public library, in an edition illustrated with many woodcuts. I was still too young to read it myself—later it became one of my favorite books—but Yan told me the story, as a kind of running serial, made more concrete to me by the woodcuts of Thornfield, of Mr. Rochester, of Jane herself, and, most exciting of all, of Mr. Rochester's mad wife in the attic. *Jane Eyre* dramatized the classic situation of the governess. Jane, like Yan, inhabited an ambiguous sphere: she was better-educated than the cook or the cleaning women, more skilled in certain areas than her employers, yet not treated fully as their social equal.

But while Yan may have identified with Jane Eyre's position, she was not in love with her employer, as Jane was; she was in love with a man named David, an artist who lived in New Hope, Pennsylvania, an hour away. She would talk to me about him a lot, when we were alone. David was married but separated from his wife, a Roman Catholic who would not give him a divorce, he told her. Yan was sure the wife would eventually give in, leaving David free to marry her. By that time, she said, I would not need her any more, so I was not to worry. I did worry secretly, not about abandonment but about Yan's happiness. Did love always churn people up this way? Was it always such a misfortune? Jane Eyre's story had ended happily ("Reader, I married him"), why couldn't Yan's?

Grandpa used to say that Yan was a "poor picker," and he was right. Perhaps her desire to care for people, which made her such a good nanny, led her to men who needed looking after. She was wooed for a while by a young Army officer named Bassler, whose intentions were honorable, according to my parents—but she just wasn't interested in him. Bassler was too much of a straight arrow for her tastes. "It's the rascals you remember," she used to say, and I still hear her saying it, with the long British "ah" in the first syllable. David's wife conveniently died before there was any divorce, but once liberated, David married someone else, a woman Yan had not even been aware of. She was heartbroken. For many weeks after the dreadful letter, I would go to her room after I was supposed to be in bed and find her crying. I was astounded by David's treachery. My parents' devotion to each other, and the books I had read so far, had led me to assume that love between men and women led, naturally and inevitably, to marriage and happiness. Her misery was my first exposure to the hazards of romance, a revelation and a warning.

Yan was luckier in one respect than Jane Eyre, who had no fellow-governesses to socialize with. Fortunately, there were some in Chestnut Hill, in particular Miss McNeill, known as Miss Mac, who looked after the Lee twins and their younger brother, Wayne; and Miss Harbor, called "Harbs," in charge of Nini and Mary Ellen ("Melon") Cook. These children were all older than I, but because of Yan's friendship with Miss Mac and with Harbs, I saw them often, heard a lot about them, and looked up to them. The first wedding I ever went to was Nini Cook's. Although Nini had long since outgrown governesses, she invited Yan and me, as well as Harbs, to the church, a memorable event. Harbs was scandalized by Nini's decision to "do all her own work," after she was married. She stayed with the Cooks in various capacities, and when she became too old to work, Nini and her husband built her a cottage on their place, where she lived out the rest of her days. Yan told me this story a little wistfully.

Miss Mac, after the Lee children were school age and she was no longer needed, left governessing and went to work as a teller in a bank branch in Suburban Station. She had an apartment in town where, as a great treat, I spent an occasional night. For years, one of my rituals was stopping to say hello to Mac at the bank when we were going into town for the dentist or a concert. When I was in my early twenties, Mac married a kind, respectable, solvent man who, according to Yan, "was going to take good care of her." They bought a house which Mac started furnishing and decorating but never got to enjoy; before they were able to move in, she and her new husband were killed in a senseless automobile accident for which they had no blame. Yan was stunned, and kept saying, "They bought a house, she was going to have her own little house, she was fixing it up." To a governess, used to living under other people's roofs, having your very own house was the hoped-for dream come true. Yan could not bear to think how close Mac had come to achieving it. By that time, Yan herself was married, though not to someone who was ever going to provide her with a house.

For eventually, she found another artist—an artisan, really—a silversmith, Mish Riggs, who lived in Rockport, Massachusetts. She met him after she had left our family and gone to look after Johnny and Carla Prizer, who lived in Chestnut Hill and whose family spent summers in Annisquam, not far from Rockport. I don't know anything about Mish's courtship, which went on over the course of two or three summers, but I do remember the wedding. The couple were married in the Prizers' garden, on a beautiful June afternoon, by a justice of the peace. Because Mish had been divorced, the Episcopal Church which Yan attended regularly would not marry them, and this was a disappointment to her. The wedding was small—just the Prizers and our family, Miss Mac and Harbs and a few other friends of Yan's. Yan wore a street length light blue dress and Mish a dark blue suit. They both seemed happy, though, and we all "hoped for the best," as my mother said privately. I could tell that my parents, even though they behaved with impeccable cheerfulness, were not at all certain that Mish was a good bet.

Yan moved to Rockport where they rented a bigger apartment than the one Mish had been living in, and found work of her own in a crafts store that specialized in enamel jewelry, which she learned to make. She got on well with the owners and with the customers. After the relative isolation from adult company that a governess's life entails, it seemed a lark to have so many opportunities for sociability. There was camaraderie and interaction among the crafts people working on the pier in Rockport. Friends would drop in for a visit during slow times and exchange news and gossip. She made a close friend, Betty Reigel, one of the craftswomen, who became her emotional mainstay and sounding board for her problems.

By the time Yan married, I was sixteen, and a year later I went to college in Cambridge, Massachusetts, so was able to drive out to see her several times a year. Even after I was married and living alternately in Washington and overseas, we kept in touch. For years I would stop overnight in Rockport to see her on my way to Maine, sometimes with my children in tow. I would stay in a nearby bed and breakfast and take Yan out to dinner at the Yankee Clipper—Mish never wanted to come along. She did not complain—this would have been against her principles—but gradually, I became aware that Yan's husband had given up any notions of supporting his wife, and that Yan was the only real breadwinner. In addition to fruit at Christmas, I took to sending her small monthly checks, made out to her alone, for which she always thanked me with embarrassing profuseness. My father also sent her monthly checks, and his and mine combined helped her to manage.

Yan came back into our lives briefly when we were getting our newly-bought house in Washington ready to rent before going to Paris for my husband Bill's first Foreign Service posting. I sent the three children, then four, two, and six months, home to Chestnut Hill for a week in order to work uninterruptedly, and Mum asked Yan to come down from Rockport to look after them. I was there to greet her when she arrived at Beechen Green. "This is like old times!" she said, and bustled around turning the guest room into a "nursery." She was shocked that baby Eliza slept in her crib with only a blanket tossed over her. "Lou! She hasn't even got a proper bed!" she exclaimed. "She doesn't get cold," I defended myself. "She sleeps in a trundle-bundle." (This was a zippered bag made of blanket material.) Yan gave me a look, went to the attic to find the old percale crib sheets, and made up Eliza's bed properly, with the top sheet folded neatly over the blanket and tucked in. "There," she said with satisfaction. Standards had been restored. After I had gone back to Washington, she went to work on the boys' table manners, and a mere seven days later, they had noticeably improved. Temporarily.

Mish and Yan stayed together until she died in her mid-seventies, of emphysema. The last time I visited her, she told me that the doctor had said to her that if she didn't stop smoking, she would die. She was defiantly smoking cigarette after cigarette., hastening her own death, willfully. Life had ceased to become enjoyable: Betty Reigel had died the year before. The owners of the enameled-jewelry shop had moved to Florida, as had several other of her Rockport contemporaries. She was working as a salesperson in a small sweater store and no longer had the cachet of being part of an artistic enterprise. She, who had always been a regular and fast walker, committed to fresh air and exercise, sat on her little green loveseat, breathless even without moving. Mish, who smoked himself, was aware of the doctor's injunction but was curiously passive about Yan's refusal to obey it. "I believe in letting people alone," he said. When he was out of the room, she handed me a small item wrapped in tissue paper. It was a sizable diamond brooch. "Muzzie gave it to me," she said. "I want you to have it. You ought to have it." She paused. "I don't want him to get it after I've gone." I tried to reassure her, and myself, that she wouldn't be gone for a long time, but we both knew this to be an improbability.

Mish called a few weeks later to say Yan had died, and I flew up immediately. I was pretty sure she had deliberately smoked herself to death. She had wanted cremation and a memorial service, neither of which Mish could cope with. (Yan, by contrast, was always a coper, one of the traits which made her such a good governess.) Mish at least signed the agreement for cremation, which requires it be that of someone "next of kin." But it was I who dealt with the priest at the Rockport Episcopal Church, arranged for a spot in the columbarium, and set a date for the service a month later. I carefully measured the size of the niche in the columbarium, and during the intervening weeks, when Bill and I were in San Francisco for a few days, we picked out a Chinese celadon ceramic jar at Gump's to hold Yan's ashes.

My parents, both my brothers, Bill, and I flew up for the service. Mish almost didn't come to the church—he didn't like churches of any denomination—but the rest of us shamed him into it. There were very few others in the pews. Walter wrote a nice eulogy, finding exactly the right tone. It did not hurt our mother's feelings, yet honored Yan and the influence she had on us. Afterwards, the priest said with satisfaction that we had had "closure," smacking his lips over the word in a way that has made me forever detest it. I always meant to stop in Rockport to visit the columbarium, but I never have. And I don't know what happened to Mish, though in any case, he must be dead by now. Yan deserved better.

Yan was an accomplished seamstress. She made me a large rag doll with long hair made of yellow yarn. She was christened "Veronica," after Veronica Lake, and Yan sewed an entire wardrobe for her. I discovered her among my parents' things when cleaning out after their deaths. I didn't know my mother had saved her. She sits in her one remaining dress, with its puffed sleeves and smocked bodice but minus its buttons, reigning over what we call the "toy room" on the third floor of our Washington house. Some of her hair has come unsewed, one shoe is gone, and her pink skin has faded. She's too shabby to give to anyone, but how could I throw her away?

Ultimately, Mum had a much more important place in the lives of my brothers and me as we grew older. She read novels to us, supervised our music lessons, went over our report cards with us, arranged for our dental appointments, saw that we got to Sunday School and to the Childrens' Concerts at the Academy of Music, planned our birthday parties and drove us to other children's. More importantly, she answered truthfully deep questions about where babies come from. She confessed she did not know what happens after you die but believed something good did. Her selfless and tireless volunteer work set an example for us, as did her dedication to music. But for eleven years, it was to Yan I turned for daily comfort and guidance. The day Yan left Beechen Green for good, I shut myself in my room and cried my heart out. I was eleven, and about to start seventh grade. I knew that I had entered a new phase of self-awareness, and that I was experiencing my first real sorrow.

c h a p t e r   t h r e e

CAPE MAY

C ape May, on the southern tip of New Jersey. A "dismal spit" my mother and her friend Gladys Brownell
used to call it in private. The Jersey shore was fine
for a summer rental—we had been in a shingle cottage
in Mantoloking for two Augusts—but not for year-round
real life. My mother was used to a secluded house surrounded by greenery; she and my father had been renting
Beechen Green for about five years. She was also used
to Friday afternoon Philadelphia Orchestra concerts at
the Academy of Music, private school for me, having her
parents an hour away, friends she had known since her
schooldays, and a host of other comforts. Gladys, who
came from Boston, was used to regular attendance at the
Boston Symphony, and these two music-loving women,

catapulted into the unfamiliar role of Navy Wives, became intimate friends very quickly. There was no piano teacher in Cape May, and so my mother gave piano lessons to Larry and Ruggles Brownell, and Gladys gave them to Walter and me. They both, wisely, wanted to avoid the perils of teaching their own children.

My father, attuned to the distant rumblings of war in Europe even before Pearl Harbor, had applied to the Naval Officers' Candidates School, been commissioned, and was serving as a Second Lieutenant. The Coast Guard Station had been turned into a Naval Base, and the Admiral Hotel had been turned into quarters for bachelor officers, but there was no "post housing" for families. My parents rented a yellow clapboard house at 901 Benton Avenue, three blocks back from the beach. There were four bedrooms on the second floor and two much smaller ones on the third. Like most of the houses on the Jersey shore, it was on pilings, in case of ocean flooding. A kind of lattice enclosed the stilts to make it look less stork-like. It had an icebox that used actual ice, and a Keystone telephone. Keystone was a system entirely different from Bell, which meant that complicated negotiations had to precede calling a Bell number in Philadelphia with the assistance of a live operator.

It surprises me to remember so much, so vividly about those two years. It makes me acutely aware of how much my granddaughters will remember of their childhood, although not *what*. My overwhelming feeling in Cape May was of unaccustomed and delighted freedom, a contrast to my protected life in Chestnut Hill, where I had never gone out unaccompanied. Our Benton Avenue house was on a corner, and although at first I had to stay "on the block" when playing outside, we were surrounded by many families with children my age and eventually the boundaries were expanded. Practically next door, there was Chessie Newhall, in my class at school, whose father was also a Naval officer. Other classmates were Lois Upham, whose father ran the summer theater and Stephanie Steger, whose father headed the Chamber of Commerce. There were vacant lots to play in, and trees to climb, singing "Up we go, into the wild blue yonder!" with only a dim idea of what the song was about. "We live in fame and go down in flame, nothing can stop the Army Air Corps!"—we liked the sound of those words. There was jumping rope on the sidewalk, with all kinds of variations. In summer twilights, there were games of Kick the Can until I was, humiliatingly, summoned to a bedtime earlier than anyone else's.

Because of the influx of Navy families, there were at least twice as many children enrolled in the local public elementary school as there had been before the war, and the faculty found it hard to rise to the occasion. In second grade, the teacher stuck out the year, but in third, there were around 40 children in my class and a series of teachers who couldn't take the chaos and quit after a few weeks. The only other school available in town was the convent school with a high wall around it, and my parents would threaten me with that now and then, when I was acting what Yan called "too big for my boots." But I knew instinctively that their fears of my becoming Catholic were stronger than their desire for a disciplined class-room and did not take these threats seriously. I'd heard my mother say, "If the nuns get you before you are eight, you are theirs for life." I already knew they were Protestant to the core, and Low Church at that.

At the start of second grade, I was six years old—"young for my class"—and everyone else was seven, except for a boy named Jimmy. I couldn't wait for my April birthday, when I would be seven too. On April 15, I announced my new age joyfully, only to discover that by then almost everyone else besides me and Jimmy had turned, or was about to turn, eight. This was a great disappointment. Although I now understood that all children got older with each birthday, not just me, I did not know for several years that this applied to grownups too, and kept reporting my mother's age as twenty-six until she was in her thirties, which occasionally embarrassed her: it meant, when I was ten, she would have been sixteen when she had me. In third grade, I was allowed to walk to and from school with my friends, out of sight of the house, which made me feel very grown up. There were probably policemen at the crossings watching over us, but I didn't notice them.

In Cape May, for the first time, I became aware of black people, and of segregation. This can't be right, but in my mind's eye, I see the "colored school" as right next to ours, separated by a chain link fence, so that during recess, we could see the colored children playing on the other side of it. Certainly the school was separate, but surely it would not have been where we could see it. Curiously, the high school was integrated, according to my parents. What rationale was being applied? Or did not many black kids make it to high school so that the small number of them didn't matter?

"Colored" was considered the polite word then, by black as well as white; the term African American had not yet been coined. There had been no "colored" in our daily lives in Chestnut Hill. In Cape May, however, the cooks, when we had them, were all dark skinned. They did not live in the house, like Mary Ann in Chestnut Hill, but arrived on weekday mornings and departed at the end of the afternoon. We ate dinner later than most Cape May families, which meant that Mummy and Yan served and washed up, and I was supposed to help. I remember two of the cooks. One was Zarina, who smoked a pipe and drove a model-T heated in winter by a wood-burning stove. Her mother had heard of the Empress of Russia and called her baby Zarina because "she was a pretty as a little Czarina." Another was Ruth, called "Luth" by three-year-old Walter, a large, soft, entirely lovable woman to whom I assigned no age but who was probably in her fifties. We went to visit her once, when she had been sick, and I remember being quite shocked by the "colored part of town." I had never known that other people's living conditions could be so different from our own. Ruth's family's house was a shack without indoor plumbing. Chickens scratched and clucked in the dirt yard. Yet Ruth herself was so lovely and kind. Why did she have to live this way? In my story books, the Good was always rewarded. Visiting Ruth was an early encounter with rank unfairness. The word "racism" was as yet unknown to me, but the concept was taking shape in my mind, as well as an association between blackness and poverty.

Then there was a black girl about my age whose name I don't remember; I'll call her Jane. Since I met her on our block, and since colored families didn't live in our neighborhood, she must have been the child of someone's live-in cook or cleaning lady. I liked her, and wanted to ask her to my seventh birthday party. My mother said No, we could not include her. She would not say why, and I could not understand her reasons, although even at the age of nearly seven, I strongly suspected it had to do with Jane's color. When I asked my mother—no racist herself—about this, many years later, she said she had been afraid that other Navy wives might have been offended by Jane's presence and kept their daughters from playing with me. She said she was sorry she had not been braver and wished she had lived up to her Quaker grandmother's ideals.

THE BOARDWALK WAS a focal point in Cape May, a source of endless stimulation for us children and for the swarms of sailors who had invaded Cape May. There were tempting things for sale: Cape May Diamonds—polished, translucent white pebbles, in rings and bracelets; salt water taffy, kewpie dolls, panda bears and teddy bears. I begged my father for a soldier doll in an Army uniform, the first male doll I had ever seen. (I undressed it immediately once home, hoping to find a penis, but to my disappointment, the doll was built just like my female dolls.). There were games of ring-toss offering the slim chance of winning a huge stuffed panda or a smaller Koala bear. There were blimps floating overhead, trying to spot German submarines. There were old people and young women and mothers with children, and young men in Navy, Army, and Marine uniforms, which we quickly learned to identify. To walk the Boardwalk was to experience the nearest thing America had to the Spanish *paseo* or Italian *pasagiatto*.

For me, the Boardwalk also had the allure of forbidden fruit, as there were so many things I was Not Allowed to Do. I was allowed to walk *on* it, as long as I had shoes on, and even to run. I was not supposed to crawl *under* it, which I did when I could get away with it, to read the discarded colored comic sections. These did not come into our house, as the adults thought that the "Dick Tracy" strip gave me nightmares. (Reading about the vicious Mrs. Pruneface when I was under the boardwalk, naturally, intensified my imagination and gave me worse nightmares.) I was not allowed to look at the penny peep shows, which were strip-teases on celluloid tape, activated when you put in a nickel. They were intended to attract the sailors, and did. Curious about their curiosity, I once stood on tiptoe when no one was looking and dropped in my nickel to find out what was interesting the sailors so much. Because I was too short to turn the crank, the pictures plopped down one by one, a slow-motion effect. By today's standards, it was a pretty innocent strip-tease; in the last image, the girl had on a bikini bottom and had turned her bare breasts coyly to one side so that you could only glimpse one of them. Why was *that* something people paid money to look at?

And I was not allowed to shoot at the moving line of tin Japanese soldiers in the shooting gallery, even though my weekly twenty-five cents would have covered it. My parents, though staunch patriots, were horrified at the substitution of caricatured enemy soldiers for the usual ducks. Mum and Dad, bless them, hated any kind of hate-mongering, and I believe I was even told not to say that I hated Hitler, though this stricture changed further into the war. When I announced to some fellow second-graders that I did not hate Hitler, my remark caused such an uproar that I was almost permanently ostracized and had to recant in order to be re-accepted. "I do *so* hate Hitler!"

My parents were both Episcopalians, as were their mothers, but both of their fathers were Quakers. Yet my father's father had died when Daddy was only five and Grandpa, my mother's father, was a Friend in name only. He went with his wife to the Episcopal church, only occasionally and only to please her. On both sides, though, each of my parents had had a set of *grandparents* who were practicing Friends. Perhaps it was their influence that made my parents determined to do what they could to prevent the inevitable prejudices that accompany wartime from seeping into my soul.

Nonetheless, Mum and Dad, and Yan too, were always on the alert to the "bad influences" of Cape May. They thought they detected a nasal "Cape May accent" infecting my speech and strove to fend it off by insisting I pronounce certain words as they themselves did. They let me take tap dancing lessons with the other second and third graders, given by Jerry Love, a pretty young woman with a halo of permed blonde hair. But I was not permitted to take part in the culminating event, the Kiddie Show, which took place in a hall on the Boardwalk sometime in May. "But why not?" I pleaded. "Why not?" I could not understand why my parents might object to a group of costumed and made-up little girls tapping away before an audience of raucous, beer-drinking young sailors and singing,

> "Oh would you like to swing on a star,
> Carry moonbeams home in a jar,
> And be better off than you are,
> Or would you rather be a pig?"

They did not really offer an explanation, I suppose because they did not want to be in the position of seeming to look down on the parents who were fine with the Kiddie Shows, even though, of course, that was exactly the position they were in. "Everyone else is in it!" I would protest, and the answer was always, "You are not everyone else. You are Louisa *Foulke*"—with an emphasis on the word *Foulke* . That was the best I was going to get. (I did hear Yan and Mum muttering to each other, "Nail polish on little girls! Mascara and eye shadow!" so I had some inklings of the reasons for their disapproval.) Stephanie Steger, whose father, as I have said earlier, was head of the Chamber of Commerce, was not only a star in the Kiddie Shows but was also "Queen of Cape May" and rode on a float in a parade, wearing a crown and a white feather cape. Oh, how I aspired to the incandescent glamour of being the Queen of Cape May, a glamour forever denied!

Whatever else was going on in the foreground, the War was always the backdrop, and young as I was, I was aware of Allies and Axis, and looked at the headlines of the newspaper. I pictured these two teams, Allies (good) and Axis (bad), in two lines facing each other. Sometimes the Allies advanced (good) and sometimes they retreated (bad). I knew that Navy fathers of some of my friends were shipped out to dangerous places, and that mine might be too. Walter and I knew that silver stars on the flags in the windows stood for sons in the armed services, and that gold stars represented ones who had died in the War. Our grandmother Foulke had two silver stars on her flag, one for my father, one for my Uncle Pardee, but it was the gold star mothers that people spoke of reverently.

Walter and I were enlisted in the War Effort too. We planted Victory Gardens in the back yard, mostly radishes and carrots, which tended to do well without much attention. We collected tinfoil from chewing gum wrappers, rolled them into balls, and put them in a special box at school, feeling useful and virtuous.

The word "sacrifice" was used a lot. Some things were rationed, and there was much talk about points, which you needed to buy sugar and meat, and gasoline. In Chestnut Hill, our parents had owned two cars, but in Cape May only one. My grandmother Muzzie referred to automobiles as "motors," and for a long time, I thought the line from "Coming in on a wing and a prayer" which went: "Though there's one motor gone, we can still carry on" referred to this necessary reduction in the Foulke family vehicles. My parents, Yan, and even Muzzie, when she came to visit, rode bicycles unless it was raining hard or there were groceries to carry. Yan, being British, was well-used to bicycle riding, and to wartime privation; she remembered World War I, and that every day a child came to school weeping because a father had died.

We sometimes bicycled, as a family, to beaches less crowded than the one along the boardwalk, Walter riding in a seat on the back of Daddy's bike. I remember once going to a place which had the reputation of having once been a cove where pirate ships anchored, and where there might still be buried treasure. (It was also relatively free of the tar from the ships which infested most local beaches; when we came back from our usual spot, close to the house, Yan or Mum had to clean our feet with cold cream.) The Brownell family was along, and Mummy and Mrs. Brownell kept urging me to dig in a particular spot on the beach. "You never know what you might find," they said, exchanging significant looks which gave away the game. I went along with this, dutifully dug, and unearthed a paper bag containing several pieces of glittering costume jewelry. The two mothers exclaimed, "Pirate treasure!" and I pretended I thought it was, because I knew that would make them happy.

IN THE FALL of 1942, my youngest brother was born, when I was six and a half. I remember being very interested in my mother's pregnancy and enjoying feeling the baby kick. There had been much discussion about what he or she should be named, and my mother had favored Gwillim, the Welsh form of William, for a boy, and Gwenlyen for a girl, to honor my father's Welsh ancestry. Gwillim could be called Gwill for short, and Gwenlyen Gwen. But in the event, he was christened William Green Foulke III, after my father, and called Billy for short.

My mother went to Philadelphia for his birth, leaving Walter and me with Yan and my father. In those days, women who could afford it were encouraged to stay two weeks in the hospital and to have a lengthy period of rest at home afterwards. Mum chose to have this postpartum recovery at her parents' house in Philadelphia, and since this lasted a month, the new baby was six weeks old before I met him.

The baby was to have my room, and I was moved to the third floor. This was presented to me as a promotion— I was now a big girl, old enough to sleep on the third floor by myself. Children are not easily conned; I was suspicious of the rationale given, and often afraid to go into the windowless bathroom alone at night—I was afraid I might see Mrs. Pruneface's body there. Even so, I was wild to see my new baby brother and could hardly wait until the day he came home. (I was much more interested in *his* arrival than in the return of my mother.) Walter, at three and a half, was developing a strong will and resisted being bossed around; I looked forward to having another sibling who would be smaller and more malleable. I imagined him as fun to play with. I pictured a baby of about year and a half—after all, it seemed like nearly that long since my mother had departed for Philadelphia.

The day mother and baby were due home, I can remember standing on the sidewalk for what seemed interminable hours, waiting for the car. When the home-coming group finally arrived, I was stunned by the reality of a six-week-old infant, a tiny red-faced bundle. Clearly, it would take a very long time for this tiny, mewling thing to be capable of play. I felt deeply betrayed.

And Billy cried a lot. My mother explained that little babies had to cry in order to develop their lungs, the received wisdom of the day. Sometimes when I was reading in my third-floor room, I would feel so annoyed by his pointless wailing that I would rush downstairs to Billy's crib and scold him. Occasionally, I would even shake him—a memory that chills my blood, knowing now what shaking can do to a baby. Fortunately, he was not damaged, and grew into a sweet-natured, cheerful child who did not remember my nastiness, and later became a sweet-natured, cheerful man whose friendship I value, along with that of Walter, who ceased being a pest and evolved into a wonderful companion.

THE AFTERNOON THE hurricane began, it seemed like just a big September storm. The sky became very dark, and rain came down harder and harder. The wind rose and began blowing the blossoms off the hydrangeas in the front yard and bent the saplings on our street nearly double. Mum was upstairs with Billy, who was only two. Walter and I were with Yan in the kitchen, where she was making a pineapple-upside-down cake, a dessert that for me, will forever be associated with that day.

"What's an upside-down cake?" I asked. "The brown sugar and butter and pineapples go on the bottom," said Yan, "then you pour on the batter, and when it's cooked, you turn it upside down, so that all the brown-sugary stuff is on top." I had been allowed to beat the batter, and Walter was licking the bowl. I looked out the window and realized that the water was up at the window level on the first floor. The house, like the other houses in Cape May, was on pilings, so this meant a depth of perhaps 10 feet. We were in the middle of an adventure; Walter and I were beside ourselves with excitement. We could hardly believe our good fortune. "Hooray! A flood!" we shouted, beginning to tear around the house. Walter began to sing his favorite song, "Pistol-packing Mama, lay that pistol down." "Stop that, please," said my mother, looking worriedly out the window at the rising water. "Why?"

asked Walter, but was given no answer. Why were the adults so unenthusiastic?

My mother told me much later that when she looked out an upstairs window that afternoon, she saw a great wall of water advancing inward from the beach some four blocks away, and like anyone in such circumstances, became scared of what might happen next, but her instinct was to appear calm in front of her children.

I heard my mother on the telephone to her mother in Philadelphia, in a low voice. I could hear her say, "too much like newsreels." When she'd finished talking, she said we'd better see if the roof was leaking anywhere. Walter and I dashed around importantly from room to room and discovered that the roof of the enclosed porch was leaking in three places. We got dishcloths to wipe up the water and put saucepans under the leaks.

My mother opened the cellar door to see how high the water was there. Only three cellar steps out of a dozen were showing. Storm doors and windows, a stepladder, the ironing board, Walter's red wooden wagon, and a number of cardboard cartons were floating. "Oh, Lord," she said, the nearest she ever came to an expletive in front of us. "All my lovely cartons I was saving!" (Cardboard boxes were in short supply, and she needed them to send food to English friends.) "I can help, Mummy," I said, hauling out the red wagon, which dripped all over the kitchen floor. Water began coming in under the front door. "Do you think we'll have to swim for it?" I asked eagerly. (I was a pretty good swimmer.") "I most certainly do not, "said my mother. "Now don't be silly and help me put newspapers down in this hall to soak up the water." Something to do, and we did it.

"The cake!" Walter said suddenly. We all rushed to the kitchen, including Yan, who pulled it out of the oven and turned it out onto a plate. "Just in time!" my mother cried, and immediately all the lights went out, as if she had pronounced a spell without realizing it. "Well, I'm glad at least the stove is gas," she said, and went for the phone to check in with a neighbor. But the phone had gone dead.

I looked out the window, pleased to see that the water showed no sign of receding. All the familiar boundaries had disappeared or changed. Our yard had no hedge around it anymore, and the crate my mother's piano had arrived in, which Walter and I had used as a playhouse, floated around over what used to be the Victory Garden. The seesaw Walter and I had bought half of with our own saved-up money had escaped into the mainstream and was floating down Benton Avenue in company with trash cans and uprooted plants. Suddenly the best thing of all sailed by: an entire segment of boardwalk, complete with a lamppost. Two grinning young men in Beach Patrol raincoats were riding the boardwalk fragment as though it were a raft. It caught on a sapling in front of our house and one of the Beach Patrol men grabbed the tree and tried to shake their craft loose. Benton Avenue had very few trees and my mother was furious at the prospect of losing one of them. She raised the window high and shouted into the wind, "You boys"—she tended to call all misbehaving men "boys"—"let go of that! Don't you *dare* break that tree!" The Beach Patrolmen looked startled, but let go the tree. The wonderful piece of boardwalk disengaged itself unaided and proceeded majestically on down Benton Avenue, the two Beach Patrolmen clinging to the lamp post.

Once it was out of sight, we remembered that we had no lights. My mother got the box of candle ends always ready for such an emergency and allowed me to hold a lighted match under each before sticking it on a saucer, something my father had taught me to do. Walter and I stationed ourselves on chairs placed back side forward, in front of the dining room window. "Not too close, in case a pane breaks," said my mother. We knelt on the chair seats grasping the backs as if they were ship railings. Night was falling, but it was not too dark for us to see a man come rowing up Benton Avenue in a big red-and-white Coast Guard lifeboat. Almost as good as the piece of boardwalk! My mother waved to him; the Coast Guardsman held the oars under his knees so that he could cup his hands and bellow, "Hey lady! You wanna be evacuated?"

"Yes!" I shouted joyfully. "Hush," said my mother, and to the Coast Guardsman, "Do we need to be?"

"Maybe," he shouted back. "Have to take care of the people on Beach Street first. Someone'll come by here in an hour, hour and a half, to check..." He was swept on before we could hear the rest. My evening job was to pull down the blackout shades, so I did that, and then we had supper by candlelight. The cake, still warm and sticky sweet, was dessert. Afterwards, I went to pack, in case we were evacuated. I went up to my third floor room, took my blue doll blanket and spread it out on my bed. I put on it my Cape May diamond ring, bought for me on the Pier by my father; my tap shoes; my trading cards; the rhinestone pin that had been passed off as buried treasure; the Classic Comics of *The Count of Monte Cristo* and *The Three Musketeers*; and my secret supply of saltwater taffy. I tied the four corners of the doll-bed blanket and put on my boots, raincoat, and rain hat. A great gust of wind suddenly smacked my middle window, which was not hooked shut, and literally blew it off. Wind and rain swept into my room. I grabbed my blanket and flew downstairs to tell. "I have no more window!" My mother looked at my outfit, asked me where I thought I was going, and told me to take it off, for heaven's sake, and get ready for bed. She went up to put cardboard over the window space in my room and told me to sleep in Walter's room that night. There was an extra bed there.

The wind died down, and, lying awake in our beds, Walter and I could hear a high pitched eerie noise, a little like a chorus of muted sirens, which had probably been going on for a while. I got out of bed and went downstairs. "What's that funny noise?" "The car horns have short-circuited," said my mother. "It's nothing serious. Go back to bed." After a while, the car batteries ran down and the noise stopped. We could hear my mother playing Chopin études on the piano downstairs, and I had the idea that this music was making the waters go down. Eventually, we went to sleep.

The next morning, the violence was over. The streets were still full of gray water, but it was much lower. The neighborhood was rising to the occasion. The milkman operated out of a boat, but wore hip boots and delivered right to the door. A house painter rowed around, salvaging such wooden-handled brushes and ladders as he could find. Stephanie Steger's father, smoking a cigar and wearing a pith helmet, began running a water-taxi service. Even Zarina the cook arrived, in a boatload of maids being pushed to their jobs by a team of six delighted boys up to their chests in water. "Ain't no water where we live now," said Zarina. "It all just settin' here in this Frog Hollow of yours." She told us that even down by the train station, it was all dry now. I felt let down: so the Flood was not worldwide, after all.

Someone rowed Chessie Newhall over to our house, and we exchanged stories. I showed her my missing window and the water in the cellar, and she said there had been *much* more water in theirs. I said defensively that there had been more water yesterday. Chessie, Walter, and I played Parcheesi, and. when we got tired of that, we played Chopsticks on the piano until Yan told us to stop, we were driving everyone crazy. Our landlord came to inspect the damage done to the oil furnace, and regaled us with descriptions of the wrecked houses along Beach Street. "Please can we go and see?" I asked. "I'm afraid they will give Walter nightmares," said my mother. "I *want* to have nightmares," said Walter, which made my mother laugh, and she relented.

In the afternoon, the water was low enough so that my mother, Walter, and I could all put on boots and walk to look at the ruined cottages on Beach Street. Porches had been ripped off and roofs hung at all angles, windows had been smashed, and sometimes walls had caved in. The stores on the Pier had been swept away, and Convention Hall had no stage left, just a piece of dance floor. I was awed, but not upset. I didn't know anyone who lived in those houses.

Back at 901 Benton Avenue, my mother began making plans to leave Cape May as soon as possible for Philadelphia, where we would stay with her parents until we could move back into Beechen Green. She told us she was worried about the safety of the water—people were talking about typhoid fever—and that getting out was the smart thing to do. She and Yan somehow managed to get suitcases and trunks packed and arrange for transportation to the railroad station by a combination of boat and truck, and by the following afternoon, we left Cape May for good, taking a train to 30th Street Station in Philadelphia and from there were transported somehow to Danny and Grandpa's house at 2100 Locust Street.

I must have realized at some level that I was irrevocably leaving behind my known world, but I don't remember how I felt about it. I do remember that the train to Philadelphia was very crowded, and that we sat across the aisle from an old couple from Pierce's Point, where, they said, fifty houses were "just swept out to sea, broken up like matchsticks." I felt jealous of *their* hurricane, which had obviously been superior to ours.

MANY YEARS LATER, to celebrate their 55th anniversary, my parents took their three grown children and their eight grandchildren to Cape May for a weekend. They chose Cape May because, they said, during their wartime years there, each day was precious. Because the future could easily bring a permanent parting, "we really lived for the moment." They wanted to recover a little of that feeling, and perhaps they did. My own feelings? Only now, having written this, do I understand how difficult these years were for my mother, and how well she endured them.

MISS ZARA'S

I n April of 2007, Miss Zara's School had a reunion of everyone who was ever a student there during its relatively short life, from the early 1940s to the early '50s. As far as I know, this was its only reunion, ever. The school never had an alumni association and held its last class more than half a century ago, but it left its mark. It was a memorable, quirky place. When, in the weeks before the reunion, I ran into a couple of women who had attended Miss Zara's and asked if they were going, the reply was unequivocal: "I wouldn't miss it for anything."

Miss Zara's was an elementary school for girls in Chestnut Hill. There was only one class of fifteen girls in each grade, so the total enrollment was only about 100. I went there for some of kindergarten, all of first grade, and after we returned from Cape May, for grades four through six.

The school building was a slightly remodeled, handsome Victorian house on roughly five acres of land. It stood on a hill—the athletic field was on a slant, which made some sports difficult, especially field hockey. The former dining room was our music room, where, led by Mrs. O'Gorman, we sang old ballads and Stephen Foster songs, most of them now considered politically incorrect, and rightly so, with their references to cheerful darkies singing and weeping over massa in de cold, cold ground. Too bad Foster's tunes were so good. On the classical side, we learned how to listen to Schubert's Unfinished Symphony. This room was also where Mrs. Randall, Miss Zara's divorced sister, who worked as a school administrator, gave recitals in which she sang unintelligible arias from Italian opera, sending us into fits of barely stifled giggles.

The large parlor had been divided into a reception area and offices. The classrooms were mostly in what had been bedrooms. Kindergarten was in a separate outbuilding. The grand, formal front staircase was reserved for teachers and, as a privilege accorded only part way into the school year, for sixth graders, after they had been proved worthy of it. We were a particularly naughty class—we could not stay in line properly or refrain from talking while in progress from one class to the next—and didn't get to use the front stairs until halfway through the year.

Miss Caterina Zara came originally from Naples. ("Bella Napoli" was another song we learned with Mrs. O'Gorman, in English.) In Italy, children started school on their fifth birthday, no matter where in the year it fell; Miss Zara saw no reason to deviate from that custom. So I went to school for the first time on my fifth birthday, April 15, in high excitement, wearing a green dress and carrying a green lunchbox. In the fall, I moved on to first grade with the group. Since I was already reading, there was no reason to keep me back. I stayed "young for my class" through high school and beyond. (This was a distinct disadvantage at times, as when in seventh grade most of my classmates went to a dancing class that accepted girls according to age, not grade in school.)

Besides the green dress and the matching lunchbox, I don't remember much about kindergarten. I remember we had boys, who, curiously, were not allowed to stay for first grade. I remember looking at illustrated flash cards, and when we had French with Mademoiselle Lambert, repeating the identifying words after her, and being told I had a good accent. (This was thanks to my mother, who spoke fluent Parisian French and coached me.) In first grade, we were introduced to Dick and Jane, the perfect middle-class white children in the spotless house with the perfect mother and father, and the dog named Spot, a family familiar to most Americans of my generation. Louise Purves and I were singled out as good readers. Even as an adult, Louise would recall how annoyed she felt the day when I was sent up to second grade to show off my skill and *she* was sent down to kindergarten to read to younger children.

Most of what I remember about Miss Zara's is from fourth through sixth grades, after the Cape May interlude. When I came back to fourth grade, cliques had been formed, and I was in none of them. There was no uniform, but there was a dress code—leather tie shoes, socks, skirts, blouses with collars, cardigan sweaters. My mother made me wear tights when it was cold. Nobody else wore them, except for Mindo Eckfeldt, who was also on the fringes. Girls did not wear pants in those days, except for "snow pants," and those only when there was actual snow. I was convinced that if only I did not have to wear tights, I would have more friends. If only I lived on Seminole Avenue or St. Martin's Lane, where the popular girls lived, instead of at the very end of West Chestnut Hill Avenue! If only I were included in the ice skating expeditions to Pastorius Park, on Saturdays! If only I could skate backwards, like Leigh Strubing and Peggy Bogan!

The others had learned things in second and third grades which I had not. When we were told to make dioramas for Book Week, I had no idea what a diorama was, let alone book week, and no one—not even Miss Trout, our no-nonsense fourth grade teacher—fully explained. By the time I finally figured out that a diorama was a kind of sideways shoe box in which you were to create a scene from a favorite book, the due date was only days away, and all I hastily managed to put together was a scene from *Sarah Crewe.* I chose for its simplicity the attic room to which the heroine is banished when she becomes a charity student, after the death of her parents from cholera in India. This I sparsely furnished with broken dollhouse furniture, to give it an aura of poverty. I did not get a ribbon. In fifth grade, we were to dress a doll as a character, and I did a little better, with Amy from *Little Women*, in green velvet, the dress sewed directly on the doll. Still no ribbon, though.

I did achieve a grudging respect for my good marks, but was never class president; holding that office was the ultimate sign of acceptance. In order to give more people a turn, and following Parliamentary Procedure, we had new elections every month, but even so, I never made it. Everyone liked Martha Denniston, who was president several times. The good athletes, especially those who played field hockey, were the school aristocrats, and I was no good at this sport. I played left wing, mostly, and the ball usually rolled on down that slanting field past me and over the goal line, to the disgust of my teammates.

Fortunately, there was a lot of emphasis on drama, for which I did have a flair. Jennie Brown and I shared the role of Beethoven in a play about his life—we both took piano lessons, which was why Mrs. O'Gorman picked us—but I can't remember now whether Jennie was Young Beethoven and I was Old Beethoven going deaf, or the other way around. We also did a non-musical play called *Ling Tang and the Lucky Cricket*. I wanted the role of Ling Tang, of course, but Anne Miller got that, and I had to be satisfied with playing one of his kite-flying friends. I did get the lead in the fifth-grade musical play called "Come to the Fair," performed outdoors. I played a poor girl who sold little bags of lavender at a country fair and had a song. ("Who'll buy my lavender, my swee—hee-heet lavender? Who'll buy? Who'll buy?") Unbeknown to all, in one of my little bags was hidden a gold coin, and whoever bought it would marry the Prince, played by Joan Ingersoll riding a real horse, her own, brought from home. Jennie Brown played a gypsy fortune teller, and when I wanted to pay for my fortune with a bag of lavender, she was to fling it on the ground and say, "Take your old lavender!" The bag was supposed to break and the gold coin was to fall out for me to claim. In the performance, the bag did not break on cue, and Jennie had to stamp on it several times, repeating "Take your old lavender!" before it released the lucky coin. I rode off with Joan Ingersoll on her horse, feeling dizzyingly high above the ground. Looking back on "Come to the Fair," which I hugely enjoyed, I realize that the story made no sense at all. Why would a prince set himself up as a randomly awarded prize? Who put the gold coin into the lavender bag? Maybe I have forgotten a crucial plot element.

MY GREATEST TRIUMPH came in sixth grade, when I won the Poetry Contest. This was a poetry-*reciting* contest: we were judged on Memorization, Pronunciation, Enunciation, Expression, Poise, and Voice. It was open only to fifth and sixth graders, although in the fourth grade we began warming up: starting then, for the next three years, each of us had to memorize a poem a week and recite it in front of the class, stating the title of the poem, the author, and his or her dates. In the fifth grade, I wanted very much to win, but lost out to Ann Miller again—she who had been awarded the role of Ling Tang the year before. Ann recited "The Wreck of the Hesperus" by Henry Wadsworth Longfellow, 1807-1882. (We had to introduce the poem with title, author, and author's dates.) I recited "The Brook," by Alfred Lord Tennyson (1809-1892) which starts "I chatter, chatter as I flow/To join the brimming river;/For men may come and men may go,/But I go on forever.") I decided that if I were to win in the sixth grade, my last chance, I would have to find something really long, preferably by Henry Wadsworth Longfellow. In my dog-eared and beloved copy of *Poems Every Child Should Know*—which I still own—I found Longfellow's "The Skeleton in Armor," a narrative poem of twenty eight-line stanzas, and decided it would fill the bill. Memory was my strong suit in those days, and I relished the task of mastering those one hundred and sixty lines.

The story was a rousing one; at the start, the poet addresses the eponymous Skeleton:

Speak! speak! thou fearful guest!
Who, with thy hollow breast
Still in rude armor drest,
Comest to daunt me!
Wrapt not in Eastern balms,

But with thy fleshless palms
Stretched, as if asking alms,
Why dost thou haunt me?"

The next stanza describes how the Skeleton starts to talk ("like the water's flow/under December's snow/ Came a dull voice of woe") and the rest of the poem is his own tale. He is, or was in life, a Viking whose story "'no Skald in song has told/ No saga taught thee"—and he instructs Henry Wadsworth Longfellow to tell it:

Else dread a dead man's curse,
For this I sought thee.

I loved the rhyme and rhythm. I loved looking up the new words in the dictionary: *skald, fen, gerfalcon, corsair.* The Skeleton is a long-winded guy, but I was crazy about all the details of his rousing, melodramatic story. He falls in love with a maiden who loves him in return, smitten by his stories of the adventures he has had. Her father refuses to give his consent to the marriage (our Skeleton is only a "Viking wild" while she is a "Prince's child"). In grand stolen-bride tradition, they run off to his waiting ship, pursued by the irate father, Hildebrand, who follows them by sea, and attacks. The Skeleton rams his new father-in-law's ship:

Down her black hulk did reel,
Through the black water!"

Then he escapes with the prince's child to a far shore, where he builds a tower that "still stands." Time dries the maiden's tears for her father, she becomes a mother, and then dies. (How? In childbirth? We are told only that "Death closed her mild blue eyes.") The Skeleton is so heartbroken by the loss that he falls on his spear. His soul ascends "up to its native stars" to a kind of Valhalla. I was thrilled by the final lines and really loaded on the Expression when I delivered them:

There, from the flowing bowl
Deep drinks the warrior's soul,
Skoal! To the Northland! Skoal!'
Thus, the tale ended.

It worked. I stunned the judges into submission. The silver cup was mine—small, but sterling, and the only cup I ever won. It sits on my bureau and I keep it polished. I can still recite chunks of the poem, though for my family's sake, I try not to.

There was a dark side to all this poetry business. The obligatory weekly poetry recitations were enjoyable, or at least tolerable, to most of us. We could choose our own poems, though the teacher had veto power. But for Robin Boyer, who was chubby and shy, recitation was a torment. She could not stand up in front of the class to say anything, at any time, without starting to cry. In the fourth grade, realizing how much Robin suffered, practical Miss Trout would ask her to come up and whisper the poem to her privately while the class was otherwise engaged. Mrs. Grafly, in the fifth grade, was kindness itself, and required Robin only to write out her weekly poem. But Miss Chandler, our sixth-grade martinet of a teacher, was determined that there be no exceptions.

Every week, Robin had to take her turn in front of the class, choking out the words of the shortest poem she could find, usually something by Emily Dickinson, tears rolling down her round, pink, face. Sometimes she broke down altogether and stood there, racked with sobs, while Miss Chandler tapped her pencil ominously on her desk and the rest of us looked anywhere but at Robin and prayed silently for her liberation. It never occurred to us to challenge Miss Chandler's cruelty and defend Robin; Miss Chandler was Authority, and we were flat-out afraid of her.

Robin's revenge was that, in her late teens she lost weight and developed into a stunningly beautiful and wildly popular young woman, courted by the son of the Aga Kahn, among others; in her twenties, she became a fashion model, much photographed for glamor magazines. I wonder if Miss Chandler ever saw Robin's lovely face in *Vogue* and had a twinge of guilt. Probably not—it's more likely she thought she'd contributed to Robin's success by toughening her up. Likelier still, to judge from Miss Chandler's own clothes—long, button-fronted dresses in drab grays and browns, high black tie shoes—is that she was supremely indifferent to magazines of *Vogue*'s ilk and never opened them.

Not so Mademoiselle Lambert, dark-eyed, young, and volatile. Despite both the lack of an appreciative male audience and the prevailing Chestnut Hill dowdiness imperative, she dressed with great care, rearranging daily the elements of her limited wardrobe and varying her look with bright silk scarves arranged in chic and mysterious ways unknown to Anglo Saxons. Her dark, bouncy curls contrasted sharply with the gray buns of the other teachers. She had fled Rouen during the war and often told us passionately about the sins of *Les Boches*, including the destruction of the Cathédral de Rouen. Although the war was over, children in Europe were still hungry, and Mademoiselle occasionally collected money for milk *pour les enfants de Rouen*.

My mother approved of Mademoiselle's accent. I inferred from other things I overheard her say that Mademoiselle Lambert had never been a teacher before coming to Chestnut Hill, and that Miss Zara had hired her because she was a refugee and genuine French person who could introduce us to French culture as well as the language. She taught us many things that French children learn: the *Fables of La Fontaine* (more recitation), verb conjugations, dictée, the principal rivers of France (La Seine, La Dordogne, La Garonne, La Rhone, La Saône) and the major mountain ranges (les Vosges, le Massif Central, les Pyranées, les Hauts Alpes, les Alpes Maritime), and the first verse of *La Marseilleise*, which we found stirring and sang with gusto. (A*ux armes, citoyens! Formez vos battalions!* We imagined ourselves, in men's attire, waving red flags and storming the Bastille.) While not mean like Miss Chandler, Mademoiselle Lambert was impatient and given to frustrated outbursts in French, mostly over our pronunciation. We had a very hard time with the "u" and the "r" and therefore never did very well with her home town, Rouen, our version of which provoked many a "Zût, alors!" To get back at her, we would ask her to say the word "thatched," which she inevitably pronounded "tash." We loved it.

On Friday afternoons, if our parents paid extra—and they all did—she taught us French Sewing. We made decorative borders on beige guest towels and the like, to be presented to mothers and grandmothers at Christmas and on Mother's Day. (My grandmother Muzzie, who loved all things Gallic, was ecstatic when she heard about the class: "Not just sewing, but *French* sewing!") In fact, I was pretty bad at any kind of sewing, as the experience of sewing Amy March's velvet dress had demonstrated. One of us was chosen each Friday to read aloud to the sewers instead of actually sewing, and I managed to finagle that role more often than not. I remember reading most of *Janneke's Island*, a novel about a Dutch girl in the early days of Nieuw Amsterdam. Strawberry blonde Louise Purves was still my rival in reading, and I remember having an unworthy ping of happiness when I learned, at the end of fifth grade, that she was moving to Mexico with her family for two years, leaving me with a clear field as lecteur.

Mademoiselle Lambert intrigued me. Unlike the other teachers, she was clearly eligible for a social life outside school. One day, bored in class, I drew two pictures of her. In one, she wore a severe suit and a scowl, and had a bubble coming from her mouth with something like "Merde, alors!" in it. This I labeled "Mlle. Lambert at school." The second, entitled "Mlle. Lambert on a date" showed her in high heels and a low-cut dress revealing daringly exaggerated breasts. Her lips were bright red and in her gloved hand, she held a cigarette in a long, black holder. When I showed the pictures gleefully to Sally Dam, who was sitting next to me, I was caught, and the incriminating drawings confiscated. As soon as the bell rang, Mademoiselle Lambert quick-marched me down to the Principal's office. "Why did you do this, Louisa?" Miss Zara kept asking me. "Why did you do this?" I could only mumble, quite truthfully, that I didn't know. I would not have been able to articulate what is obvious to me now: that I wanted to amuse, to gain friends by amusing. My punishment was mild—possibly Mademoiselle Lambert was secretly flattered and interceded for me. I had to apologize, in laborious and misspelled written French, to Mademoiselle, and perhaps I had to stay late after school. One effect was a conscious resolution to avoid getting caught in the future; my life as a quiet subversive had begun.

What else can I retrieve about Miss Zara's? The year I graduated, 1947, is a long way back. Flotsam and jetsam: The yellow mini-van that took classmates and me to school in the morning, driven by a patient and long-suffering Miss Wood in thick glasses. Field Day in the spring, wearing blue shorts (we were assigned to either the Blue or the White team) and surprising myself and others by doing well enough in the broad jump to earn a ribbon. Ceramics class, and making a small, successful black glazed swan for my grandfather, and also a disastrous what?—rabbit? cat?—which exploded in the kiln, having been insufficiently hollowed out. Painting a long group mural on brown butcher paper depicting Early Man's daily life. I was responsible for a standing man painting on the wall of a cave. I painted first the horned animal he was drawing, then the man's head and body, which turned out to be so much lower down than his art work that I had to give him a disproportionate ape-like arm long enough to reach it. Writing a research paper on Florence Nightingale and being struck by her courage and resourcefulness. Oral quizzes in Greek and Roman Ancient History, with the emphasis on Greek. We would stand at our desks while Miss Chandler went across the rows asking a question to each girl in turn. If you got the answer wrong, you had to sit down, and she who was left standing at the end won. How did Socrates die? (Drinking hemlock.) What city was the chief rival of Athens? (Sparta.) Who ran to Sparta before the Battle of Marathon to ask for help fighting the Persians? (Phidippides.) When was the Golden Age of Greece? (500 BC.) Who learned to orate by filling his mouth with pebbles and speaking by the ocean? (Demosthenes.) And so on. After Louise Purves left for Mexico, I was often the winner, which did nothing to make me more popular. I had not yet learned the value of modesty.

Nevertheless, though never one of the Class Leaders or popular girls, I did have some friends during my last year and had a sense of belonging to the group, never stronger than at graduation. We stood a row on a cool, green June morning, fifteen pre-teen girls wearing knee-length white dresses, all different. The color white, the cornflower bouquets we carried, the white socks and black patent-leather Mary Janes supplied the requisite visual unity. There was a prize awarded for citizenship, which I never had a crack at, and which probably went to Martha Denniston. There were some other prizes—I may have won one for the best French *cahier*, but I'm not sure. No doubt there were speeches. I remember being puzzled by the word "commencement" on the program. I knew commencement was a beginning, and surely this was an ending.

To return to the 2007 reunion. It was held in a community arts center in Chestnut Hill, Miss Zara's physical school having been demolished long since to make room for an assortment of smaller houses. An energetic committee had set up displays of the famous hand towels embroidered in French Sewing, and artwork by those who had evolved into painters and sculptors. Around a hundred women showed up, identified by large, legible name tags. We sat at tables by graduation year. There were six of us from 1947, not a bad percentage. As we had moved in body to seventh grade at Springside School, many had been classmates through high school, and we chattered away as though a few years, not half a century, had elapsed since we were together. Basic personality traits were still visible. The girl who had always dressed well was well dressed. The indifferent student with an irreverent sense of humor still made us laugh. The one with a bossy streak still bossed.

News of Louise Purves's death had recently reached us, and saddened us all. After she and her family had returned from Mexico and Louise came to Springside, we became good friends rather than rivals. As an adult, she had turned into a distinguished translator of French into English. She'd been living in Paris, on Montmartre, with a second husband, who was French. It sounded very romantic. We wanted to know more of her story.

We agreed that Miss Zara's had had a profound influence on us all, though it was hard to pin down exactly what that influence was. Academically, Miss Zara's was of its time and place, and my granddaughters would find the blanks in the curriculum appalling. The math was limited to basic calculations and there was no real science. History was exclusively European history, except for Ancient History, which included countries like Persia. Geography was a separate subject. Yet in the realms of literature, writing, music, drama, art, and foreign language, Miss Zara's served us well. Miss Chandler aside, the teachers did no harm. Most crucially, although we did not realize this at the time, an effort was made to instill in us the belief that we were as capable as men and as important, and this, in the late 1940s, was still a novel idea.

chapter five

CHRISTMAS

The wartime Christmases we celebrated in Cape May were happy but restrained, compared to the ones in peace. Back in Chestnut Hill, the War behind us, and joyfully relieved that our life had returned to normal, my mother began pulling out all the stops. She loved every aspect of Christmas and devoted at least a month to getting ready. The brightly colored cards, usually with a religious motif, were ready to go out before Thanksgiving and always included a family photo and a poem my mother had written, encapsulating the carefully chosen news of the past year. My parents received what seemed like hundreds of cards in return, and looking at them decorating deep window sills of the tall living room windows, I would wonder how anyone could possibly have that many friends.

My mother did not think it legal to decorate the house until after December 1, but after that date, her campaign went into high gear. There was the wreath on the front door, of course, full of pine cones and tiny colored glass balls, finished off with the obligatory big red bow. On the grand piano, out of children's reach, sat a very plain, simple crèche in white plaster, bought in Oberamagau, Germany, before the War and much prized by both parents: Mary and Joseph, the Babe, and two angels sat on a box covered in silver paper. Another crèche, in carved wood, complete with wise men, shepherds, and sheep, sat on the antique spinet in the front hall. The banisters of the staircase were festooned with fragrant evergreen garlands and more red bows. The stair carpeting was its usual deep red, conveniently harmonizing with the color scheme. Mistletoe in a glass bell hung from the front hall ceiling light. I could not imagine any place more dazzlingly beautiful than Beechen Green at Christmas. I still can't.

The suspense of the final days leading up to the 25th was nearly intolerable. Sometimes there was snow, not always, but often, and we children observed the sky carefully every morning and hoped hard for a White Christmas. When it failed to snow, my mother would say cheerfully, "We're having a *green* Christmas." We all still believed in Santa Claus, or pretended to. I was at heart deeply doubtful, but kept my suspicions to myself, intuiting that more loot would be forthcoming to the believers than the scoffers.

The Sunday afternoon before Christmas, our parents—our mother, really—gave a carol-sing for the neighborhood families which became a tradition. The guests took advantage of the occasion to put their little girls in velvet dresses and wear their own party clothes. We children would pass out leaflets of the words and Mum would lead the singing and play the piano. Mum was a good sight-reader, and requests for favorites were honored, even off-center ones like "In the Bleak Mid-Winter." For "We Three Kings." Mum would ask for volunteers to sing Caspar, Melchior, and Balthazar, and for "Good King Wenceslas," the Page and the King. (I sometimes got to sing the Page, and years and years later, our oldest son sang the good King himself.) My father could not carry a tune so never volunteered for solos, but joined in bravely with the choruses. When my mother thought everyone had had enough, she would start "Silent Night." We lit candles and turned out the lights for this last one—I did not yet consider this corny. The carols were followed by refreshments in the dining room, eggnog for the grown-ups and hot chocolate for the children, Christmas cookies—square ones that tasted of licorice, and pfeffernusse, pungently spicy and dusted with confectioner's sugar.

My father enjoyed Christmas greatly too and approved of all my mother did, but did not participate in the preparations, which were women's work. He bought his Christmas presents for my mother on the afternoon of

Christmas Eve at Bonwit Teller, across the street from the Provident Trust Company. He liked having the store pretty much to himself, except for a few other husbands doing the same thing, all of them glad to be receiving the full attention of the attractive sales ladies. Mum bought and wrapped all the rest of the presents. (When we were older, Dad picked out his own presents for us children.) And she bought presents for everyone in her life. She sent Christmas packages to friends in England and France still suffering from wartime shortages. The Christmas cash tips she gave to everyone who delivered to the house were slipped into nice cards and accompanied by a package of candy tied round with a ribbon.

On the evening of December 24th, my father would read us "The Night Before Christmas," savoring every familiar word. As a family, which included Yan, we would sing a few carols together, the big folding doors to the living room from the hall, usually kept open, were shut, and would not be opened until after breakfast the next day. The tree, which Santa Claus supposedly brought with him and decorated, would appear in the morning, surrounded by packages. (More than any other fiction, the one that Santa did all this for everyone all over the world undermined my credulity, but I played along for years.) Then we would go upstairs, hang our stockings on the mantel of the fireplace in our parents' bedroom and try to go to sleep. In the morning, not a minute before six o' clock, we knocked on the bedroom door, calling "Merry Christmas!" and were told to come in. The stockings were filled literally to overflowing and usually there were "extra" things underneath them. I tried to open my stocking slowly, to show how much more mature I was than my brothers, but it was hard. Everything in it was exciting—the plastic pencil-sharpener, the dime-store bracelet, the tiny angel with real feathers on its wings, the round, flat chocolates wrapped in gold foil and stamped to resemble coins, the red and yellow barley-sugar animals. My brothers got the same candies and pencil-sharpeners, and little cars and tin soldiers as well. (I wanted soldiers too, but never got them until one Christmas many years later, my grown eldest son, having heard of my deprived childhood, gave me two, which sit on a bedroom shelf of knick-knacks.) My parents always said, as we sat happily playing with our treasures, "Stockings would have been quite enough." There would have been no need for more presents.

But there were more presents anyway, from Yan, grandparents, aunts, uncles, as well as from our parents. First we had to get dressed, next we had an agonizingly slow breakfast sitting down at the table in the dining room, and then at last the doors to the living room were opened. There was the glorious tree, decorated with lights and glass balls all in different colors and glittering silver tinfoil, and the mounds of presents under it. My parents and Yan wrote down what we had received from whom almost as fast as we could open presents, before they had touched any of their own. This way, we were primed to thank the grandmothers and aunts when they called. Not that saying thank-you over the phone excused us from writing notes: you were excused from writing only when you opened a present in front of the giver and could thank them in person.

Christmas day dinner would take place either at the house of Danny and Grandpa, my mother's parents, or at Muzzie's, my father's mother, sometimes lunch with one and dinner with the other. My mother decided she wanted to have her very own festive Christmas meal as well, so she had hers on Christmas Eve, like a French "reveillon," except that in France, the meal follows mass. We children were not included in this until we hit twelve. We had early supper overseen by Yan, who put on her best dress after we were in bed and joined the grown-up party. Mum would gather in single people and childless couples, including my father's unmarried brother, Uncle Pardee, Uncle Wharton Hipple , not a true uncle but an old friend of Grandpa's, Aunt Bert, tall and red-haired, a "courtesy aunt," interesting to me because she had a real job in an art gallery, the only one of my mother's friends to work for money. There were never fewer than a dozen at the table. The guests "dressed" for dinner: black tie for the gentlemen, long dresses for the ladies. Mary Ann cooked, and Nora served. I knew from my reading that most people did not live this way, but I did not yet question it.

The table, impressively long with its leaves in and covered with a special Christmas tablecloth embroidered with red poinsettias, was resplendent with newly polished silver, crystal glasses, Limoges place plates, all Mum's most cherished things. Silver dishes of nuts and chocolates were at both ends of the table, a porcelain bowl of red and white carnations she had arranged herself in the middle. "Favors"—small ornaments to take home— and a wrapped present were at each place.

When I was finally twelve and invited to this feast, I was suffused with happiness at being there. First came clear turtle soup flavored with sherry, in a two-handled cup. Then a plate of oysters on the half-shell. I tried one and nearly gagged, but sure I would be sent away from the feast if I did, I swallowed it, though I declined to eat the rest. My father, noting my expression, said tactfully, "Oysters are an acquired taste." Roast beef with souf-fled potatoes, and for dessert, ice cream birds, made in moulds, in edible nests of spun sugar. Turkey and plum pudding, sometimes twice, were for the next day with the grandparents.

That year, I was allowed to acknowledge that Santa Claus was a great, benign fantasy, and when my broth-ers were in bed, I helped to trim the tree and set out the presents. When I saw that Walter's and Billy's piles were bigger, I felt a pang of envy. They were loved more than I! I surreptitiously counted the presents and saw that actually, we all had the same number, and was mol-lified. The next day, I realized that the difference in the size of the pile was because my presents were no longer large toys but books, clothes, and even jewelry, all of which took up less space.

After the reveillon, I went for the first time with my parents to the eleven p.m. service at St. Thomas's Church,

Whitemarsh, the church of my father's boyhood. My parents loyally attended it all their lives, even though another Episcopal church, St. Paul's, was less than a mile away. On Christmas Eve, Mr. Groton, the rector, always gave a short, inspiring homily in the deep, resonant speaking voice he had developed from having to contend with the noise of freight trains rumbling by on a noisy nearby overpass. The organ music, the candlelight, the special choir anthems, the smell of the pine and balsam decorating the church, put me into a state of transcendence that no service has been able to reproduce since.

The first Christmas vacation back from boarding school, when I was fourteen, I saw everything with new eyes, and was filled with a genuine appreciation of everything my mother had done to surround her family with beauty. I remember the feeling of descending the staircase and pausing on the landing to admire the decorations in wonder.

I doubt that I ever thanked Mum for any of it.

My mother continued to celebrate a full-court Christmas for many years. When we three children were grown and had families of our own, two of us in distant cities, they began to celebrate with each of us in turn, always arriving with a station wagon full of beautifully wrapped presents. The Christmases she did not spend with us Newlins, she sent trinkets for everyone's stockings, in quantity, in addition to the official presents. She kept on decorating her own house, no matter where she was spending Christmas. She could not resist buying one or two new things every year—figurines of carolers, clusters of painted wooden angels, more crèches, some new bauble for the tree—which added up over the years, so that by the time she and my father moved to a smaller house, she had to give away half of the Christmas paraphernalia, reluctantly. She continued to hold the carol sing until her early eighties, when she had bypass surgery. She and my father together kept up the Christmas cards, and after her death, with the help of a secretary, he soldiered on until his death at 94. He did not attempt a poem, but he'd pick out a photo of a recent great-grandchild to include. There were still more than 400 names on the list, many of them the children and grandchildren of long-deceased friends. The secretary had to address the envelopes, but my father signed his name himself on every card. The ritual was important to him, and gave him the illusion of being in touch with a wider world.

My brothers and I gradually lost our childish enthusiasm for the Christmas experience our mother had provided. As a mother of three with a job, I resented for many years the amount of money and time my mother devoted to Christmas. I wished she would not give us so much. Maybe I was just envious of her relative leisure. Or, maybe I felt I couldn't possibly live up to her standard, which had imposed a burden on me. My brother Walter, the only one of us who remained in Chestnut Hill, associates the carol-sings that took place after he became an adult with being dragooned into moving furniture around and straining his back.

I am now ashamed of my mean-spirited rejection of my mother's generosity, grateful for the Christmases at Beechen Green in all their glory. If she expressed her love for us by buying things, which she did throughout the year, picking up things here and there that she thought would please us, if she expressed her love for her friends and neighbors with her carol sing and her Christmas Eve reveillon—is there anything really the matter with that?

chapter six

MUSIC LESSONS

M y mother loved music—almost all kinds of music, but classical music the most dearly. She was a gifted and accomplished pianist, and had been told by a teacher when she was in her teens that she was good enough to be accepted by the prestigious Curtis Institute of Music in Philadelphia. Applying there—or to any professional music school—was, however, out of the question. Her conservative parents did not want her to be a professional anything, or even to go to college. She was to marry someone favorably known to her family and become a good, cultivated, public-spirited wife and mother. Were she to go to Curtis, she might fall in love with a musician, perhaps even a *foreign* musician, a Hungarian violinist, for example. That would not have done.

Her mother, whom I called Danny, went faithfully to the Philadelphia Orchestra Friday afternoon concerts. Like the ladies with whom she lunched beforehand at the Acorn Club, she believed in the Orchestra as an institution, and in its conductor, Eugene Ormandy. Danny greatly admired Ormandy, born in Hungary, who had started his career as a child prodigy violinist. But for her daughter to *marry* anyone like Ormandy would have been unthink-able. Danny and Grandpa's family, the Woods, thought of musicians as consummately unreliable husbands. To make their case, they cited the case of Leopold Stokowski, a former conductor of the Philadelphia Orchestra , who married a series of well-off , ill-fated women. (When I was a child, he was married to Gloria Vanderbilt, wife number three, mentioned by the Woods in hushed tones as an object lesson on the perils of getting mixed up with musicians.) Mum was no rebel, even in youth; she was a third and youngest child, adored by her father, and it did not seriously occur to her to go against him or her mother and apply to Curtis.

Where Mum's passion for music or her talent came from is a mystery. Her brother Dick had a nice tenor voice and sang with a men's chorus called the Orpheus Society, and one of her first cousins sang with a local Gilbert and Sullivan company, but neither of her parents played an instrument or sang anywhere but in church. She continued to work hard at the piano even after she was a married woman with children, and she took weekly lessons for years. She said they gave her the motivation to practice. There were two grand pianos in our living room at Beechen Green, arranged so that the players faced each other and the piano tails nestled together compatibly, creating what appeared to me an unbroken expanse of piano. She often played piano music for "four hands" with one or another of her women pianist friends.

Mum was regularly invited to give recitals, for free, in places like museums, schools, and retirement communities, where she was applauded appreciatively. These recitals, like her lessons, stimulated her to "keep up her music," as her friends called it. I am glad she did. Some of my sweetest childhood memories are of listening to her playing Schubert, Chopin, Schumann, and Bach as I fell asleep upstairs. I can not tell you the names of the études, the sonatas, waltzes, and inventions, but there are passages that, when I hear them, after more than seventy years, bring back so much that they move me to tears. My father, who was literary but unmusical, was immensely proud of my mother's playing, but sometimes jealous of the amount of time it took her away from his side. It was years before I understood how lonely it must have been for her to be unable to share music with her beloved. To please her, he accompanied her to concerts after he retired, but his heart was not in it, and after her death, he canceled the subscription to the Philadelphia Orchestra series.

Mum was determined to give all three of her children a good musical education, which included the study of an instrument. When I was around five, she started me on piano lessons with her. These continued in Cape May, with Mrs. Brownell, as I have mentioned in an earlier chapter. I don't remember any major conflicts with Mrs. Brownell, though I did not make any major progress, either. The book we used is still in print: John Thompson's *Teaching Little Fingers to Play*. I got about as far as "The Scissors Grinder," the first piece which had a flat in it, and I can still hear myself hesitating before hitting that note. ("Round and round, Round and Round, Goes the wheel, when—*flat!* Scis-sors are ground. The edge is sharp, That once was flat, scis—*sharp!* sors grinders Tend to that.") I appreciated the musical puns.

Back in Chestnut Hill after the War, when I was going on nine and in the fourth grade, I was put into the hands of Miss Gillett, a teacher who gave lessons in the living room of her house on Ardleigh Street, walking distance from our house. Mum had faith in Miss Gillett: she paid attention to technique, especially to proper fingering. She discouraged the use of the loud pedal and required a religious adherence to daily, supervised, practice

Both my brothers emerged from their Miss Gillett years as accomplished pianists and still enjoy playing regularly. Unfortunately, I developed an instant antipathy to Miss Gillett and balked at learning from her. She had an incentive system which I was determined to sabotage. Each of her pupils had a notebook in which assignments for the next lesson were written. All the notebooks had to be the same, those bound black-and-white marbled stiff-covered ones that you can't tear the pages out of easily. At the end of the assigned lesson, Miss Gillett would paste a small silver star on that page of the notebook for a well-prepared lesson, and for a *good* lesson, a small gold star. Poor or indifferent preparation meant no star. Five small-gold-star lessons in a row earned you a big gold star, and five big gold stars in a row earned you a prize, chosen by Miss Gillett. *In a row!* That was what got me (Since I never made it to any prizes, I can't tell you what they were.) She threatened a red star for "losing your temper." I was curious about this red star. I suspected it did not exist, and to test my theory, I semi-faked losing my temper during a lesson and threw my music on the floor partly in frustration, partly as an experiment. My instincts proved correct: there were no actual red stars. There wasn't even a red pencil. Miss Gillett came close to losing her own temper as she angrily drew, in gray pencil, a star on the relevant page and labeled it "red," underlining the word. I felt an unholy surge of triumph, short-lived.

Miss Gillett believed in having a parent sit on the piano bench by the child while she or he practiced. It was this that finally undid me, and my poor mother too. I do not know whether it was that Mum played so well that I despaired of ever meeting her standards, or that I lacked the musical gene which luckily descended to both my brothers and two of my three children, or whether it was some other factor I have never identified, but in any case, I could not stand practicing with her beside me as coach. I rebelled angrily against being corrected. "You can't take criticism," my mother said, and she was right. I threw real temper tantrums, which ended by my slamming down the lid of the keyboard and stomping away. No amount of being sent to my room to cool off helped the situation.

My desperate mother consulted a child psychologist, by herself. The psychologist's view was that I should learn to play a different instrument, one Mum did not play. I thought that playing the accordion might be fun, but Mum said this was not what she had in mind. I needed to choose an instrument that would be welcome in a symphony orchestra.

Having already been to numerous "children's concerts" at the Academy of Music on Saturday mornings, I was familiar with some of the musicians, and liked to watch one of the flutists, Willie Kincaid, who had prematurely white hair and a very pink face, pinker still when he was playing. "What about the flute, then?" I proposed. Mum agreed in principle, but could not locate a flute teacher within a half-hour driving distance from Chestnut Hill who was both up to her standards *and* who would take beginners. She did find a Mrs. Cochran who taught violin and lived only a mile away, and this is how the violin became my instrument.

Mum wanted me to have what she called a "decent violin" on which I would have a chance of making a nice sound, and took me to William Moënnig and Sons at 2039 Locust Street in downtown Philadelphia, to choose one. The Moënnigs were makers of violins, violas, cellos, and bows, and dealt in old stringed instruments as well. William Heinrich Moënnig had come to the U.S. from Saxony at the end of the 19th century, established his Philadelphia shop in the later '30s and was revered by the musicians of the Philadelphia Orchestra and Curtis Institute. (To my astonishment, when I looked up the spelling of "Moënnig" on the internet, I discovered that the shop is still there and that the family firm is in its fourth generation of violin makers and dealers. The present generation spells the name "Moenning".) "Old Mr. Moennig," as I thought of him—he must have been in his mid 60s at the time—took this purchase for a ten-year-old seriously, and had me try out several violins and bows in Mum's price range before they agreed on what was right for me. I remember feeling happy as I walked out with my new violin and bow in their case, and also guiltily aware that this expenditure represented a real sacrifice for my parents.

Mrs. Cochran, unlike Miss Gillett, was not a martinet, which may be why I remember her less clearly. She was probably in her late forties—middle aged, middling looks, neither especially slender nor fat. She had graying curly hair and kept track of her reading glasses by hanging them on a black string around her neck, a system I hadn't seen before and have ever since associated with her. She herself loved the violin and, although kind and cheerful, her expression was a combination of hope and resignation: she knew that the chances were slim that any of her pupils would achieve the heights—but you could tell that she hoped that someday, somehow, one of them just might.

Mrs. Cochran wanted me to *feel* what I was playing. "You have to play with your solar plexus," she used to say earnestly. I wasn't quite sure where that was, even though she indicated that it was somewhere under the rib cage. Protestant herself, she said more than once that Jewish students tended to be better violin students than Protestants, "because Jewish children mature emotionally earlier." This was a novel idea to me, and reinforced the impression I had from knowing the Rosenbaum family that there were real advantages to being born Jewish, even though Mr. Rosenbaum had become an Episcopalian to counteract some of the disadvantages.

I was pleased to discover that violin music was written only in the treble clef; this made reading the music easier. On the other hand, it was harder to coax a noise out of the violin that anyone could stand listening to. With the piano, the notes just sat there in the keys, waiting to be pressed. I enjoyed the routine of self-importantly putting resin on the bow and tuning the instrument, but it was quite a while before the sounds I produced bore any resemblance to music. My mother did not stay in the room with me while I practiced, which made the switch to violin worthwhile for us both.

Eventually, I learned some "pieces," but once my "piece" had been practiced and played in a Christmas or spring recital, it went out of my fingers forever, though it remained permanently in my head. "The Swan," by Saint-Saens, was one of these, and another was "Country Gardens," an old English dance tune. The latter I learned when I was drafted to be the violinist in a dramatic rendering, at school, of Mrs. Fezziwig's Christmas party from Dickens's *Pickwick Papers.* (No one else in the school played the violin.) So I played while others merrily danced, and I began to have an inkling of how being a violinist might remove you from things that looked like much more fun.

One of Mrs. Cochran's other violin pupils was Barbara Linglebach , called "Bobbie," whose parents were friends of my parents. Mum, Mrs. Linglebach, and Mrs. Cochran arranged that I should go to the Linglebach house on Monday afternoons after school, "to play string quartets." By then, I was about thirteen and had "made progress," but I was certainly not ready for string quartets. Bobbie, though my age, was much more proficient, and played first violin. I played second, Mrs. Linglebach played the viola and another grown-up I didn't know played the cello. Mrs. Linglebach had only begun viola lessons a year earlier, though she played the piano well, sometimes with my mother. I was intrigued by the realization that an adult could be a beginner and make mistakes, like me.

I liked saying to other people that I was "playing string quartets," and there were indeed occasional moments when I was entirely caught up in the thrill of making music collaboratively, but much too often, the others would come to the end of their parts while I was still finishing up, several bars behind, kind of like coming in fourth in a race, which must have made for an odd effect for anyone listening. The other players were patient with me, but were probably relieved when I went to boarding school in the tenth grade and abandoned the Linglebach musical afternoons.

At "Farmington," whose real name was Miss Porter's School, I continued my lessons with a man who played with the Hartford symphony and came out once a week to the school, just for me. He was nice enough, but colorless and doleful. (I had begun to form the impression that all music teachers are destined for lives of disappointment and sorrow.) For the first time, I had to choose between music and art—the school's policy was to allow you to take one or the other; both might distract you too much from your homework. I had no trouble with the homework, and having to choose was annoying. Even though it would have been unthinkable to let music go, given my mother's passion and my loyalty to her, I had liked drawing and painting at Springside and was sorry to leave them behind.

For my first two years, I was, again, the only girl in the entire school who played the violin. Again I was drafted for a play, *Romeo and Juliet* this time, and was a court musician in green tights when I would much rather have been Juliet in a long red velvet dress. Or rather, *one* of the Juliets: so many of the girls wanted to play the role that in a time-honored high school tradition, Juliet was parceled out among a dozen eager young actresses.

There were three "major clubs" at Farmington: Drama, Chorus, and the Mandolin Club, so named back in the twenties when the mandolin was all the rage. No one at the school had played the mandolin for decades, but the name remained by tradition and the club had become the one for instrumentalists. The trouble was, from my point of view, that the school did not permit anyone to be a member of more than one major club. Although you "tried out" for these clubs, if more than one club wanted you, a faculty committee decided which one would get you. There were few girls who played instruments of any kind, so inevitably I became a member of the Mandolin Club and had fun writing and performing shows with the group, though I was wistful about not being able to act in a play or sing in the chorus.

During my senior year, my violin once served, blissfully, as a passport for an outing to Boston. The choral director and advisor to the Mandolin Club, was a lively young divorced woman full of humor named Mrs. Karstens, who had a real liking for adolescents She taught three of us to play a trio by Loillet—the instruments were flute, violin, and piano—to show off the school's music program to an alumnae meeting in a Boston ladies' club. The Loillet trio excursion sprung the three of us from school for an entire day and catapulted us briefly from the circumscribed village of Farmington into the intoxication of a real city. In those days, Farmington girls were not allowed into Hartford at all; seniors were permitted to go shopping in West Hartford two afternoons during the year, so getting all the way to Boston was an exciting achievement. Thanks to Mrs. Karstens, always blessedly relaxed about School Rules, we even managed to have tea afterwards with some boys we knew at Harvard, which whetted our appetites for the freedom that was to come after graduation.

My doleful violin teacher urged me to continue my lessons when I got to college, and I told him I would, but there were so many new things to try as a freshman that I never did. Actually, I did play once more, though not at college. There was an embarrassing champagne-induced moment, only dimly remembered and probably best forgotten altogether, when on a trip to Europe with three friends the summer after our freshman year, I bragged to the band leader in a night club that I had once played the violin, and he got me up on stage to play something with the others—*what on earth did we play?*—and everyone cheered.

My mother felt that she had done her best and did not pressure me to go on with the lessons. She was a realist; it wasn't as if there had ever been evidence of a striking talent. Even though I opted out, I have never regretted those seven years of lessons. They taught me an incalculable amount about music and gave me a profound appreciation of anyone who can play a stringed instrument even passably well. When we lived in Guatemala, others mocked the Guatemala Symphony Orchestra; I never did.

Although I stopped playing, I did not get rid of the violin itself. I kept thinking I might return to it some day, when the circumstances were right. I took it to Paris when I was twenty-six and going with Bill to his first Foreign Service Post. By that time we had three children, but since in Paris we could afford an *au pair* girl, it became possible for me to consider taking lessons again. In a conversation with someone knowledgeable about music, I mentioned the Linglebach String Quartet era as having been particularly satisfying, time having cast a rosy glow over those struggling afternoons. She immediately encouraged me to take up the viola, as amateur string quartets all over the city were pining for violists. She convinced me to sell my violin and buy a viola with the proceeds. Since I had always done best with the lower registers of the violin, this made sense to me. Little did I know.

I sought out the Paris street almost entirely given over to shops selling stringed instruments of different kinds, the Rue de Rome in the 9th *arrondissement*, which required a couple of metro changes. My knowledgeable friend had named a particular shop, and there I went with my Moënnig violin. The dealer was impressed by my violin's provenance and gave me in even exchange a viola that sold for twice what my parents had paid for my violin. I returned to our apartment on the Avenue Mozart well pleased with my prize.

But then there were the lessons. Two unanticipated problems emerged right away: (1) although my French was good, it wasn't good enough for viola lessons; and (2) the music was written in the bass line, in what the teacher called the *"clef d'ut."* This key was identified in the Petit Larousse as the key of C, and in the Harrap's English-French dictionary as the key of *fa*, and this confused me, since I had always thought that *do* was C. Whatever key the music was written in, I could only read it slowly and hesitatingly, note by painful note. My teacher wanted me to learn solfège, which he thought essential to mastery of any instrument, and I made a pass at this without success. The whole process was too hard for me. I did not have the motivation to persevere. I realized after a few months that in the time left to us in Paris, I was never going to be welcomed joyfully into a string quartet lacking a violist, and stopped the lessons.

Nevertheless, when we returned to the United States the viola came with me. But I decided that if I was ever going to play a stringed instrument again, it would be the violin after all, the music for which I could, at least, read. I figured that I could again trade up. The franc-dollar exchange rate was then in our favor. I made a pilgrimage from Washington to Philadelphia, to Mr. Moënnig's shop, still on Locust Street. The original Mr. Moennig had died three years before—this would have been in 1965—and his son was now in charge. "A very fine instrument," he said of the Paris viola. "You did well." In another even exchange, he gave me a violin priced at double the worth of the viola. I told my mother that in the process of my trading up, her original monetary investment had now quadrupled.

You will have already guessed that this final violin languished in its case, atop the piano, like its predecessor. Maybe I took it to our next foreign post, Guatemala, maybe not, but I certainly didn't do anything with it there, nor during a long post in Washington after that, when I was teaching and in graduate school. Finally, cleaning out the house in preparation for our third foreign assignment, in Brussels, I faced reality and decided to give the violin to the DC Youth Orchestra, a worthy organization which at the time of this writing still exists. It provides both lessons and instruments to young people who could not otherwise afford them. That marked the end of my long, ambivalent relationship with the violin, but there is a nice postscript to the story.

Years after I had donated the violin to the Youth Orchestra and we were once more in Washington, Bill was filling a prescription at our local pharmacy, which was still a People's Drug Store before the CVS takeover. "Newlin," the pharmacist said thoughtfully. "Is that any relation to the Newlin Violin?" It turned out that her son played in the DC Youth Orchestra and had the privilege of playing the violin we had donated. We were pleased to learn that the instrument was still being used and appreciated, but were taken aback to learn that it was identified by our name. I wonder if someone is still using it, and if it is still called the Newlin Violin. I like to think it is, but don't want to investigate, in case it isn't.

chapter seven

NORTHEAST HARBOR

Is it because I came to this particular Maine village when I was a baby that it has always had a powerful hold on my feelings? I was sent to Northeast Harbor in 1936, when I was three months old, to stay for the summer with my grandmother Foulke, "Muzzie." She had hired Miss Smith, a young English nanny, to look after me for the summer. (Miss Smith, called "Yan"—no one remembers why—ended up staying eleven years.) My young parents, twenty-one and twenty-three, had sailed off for England, to be in the wedding of one of my father's best friends, and I was thought too little to make the trip, and too inconvenient to have along. I have been coming to Northeast Harbor for at least part of almost every summer since then. Not during most of the World War II years and not during some of Bill's Foreign Service postings, but mostly.

After Muzzie died in 1951, her house was sold and passed through the hands of several owners over the next twenty-six years. When it came up for sale in 1976, Bill and I bought it back, and now, astonishingly, we have had it for longer than Muzzie did. I am unreasonably attached to it. The dry pine scent of wood fires in the fireplace and the damp smell wafting up from the earth floor of the basement when you open the cellar door to the steep stairs down, take me back six and more decades. The house has been called "Four Winds" since Muzzie acquired it in 1927 as a dilapidated wreck and restored it.

The name is not very original, but it's accurate; Four Winds sits on the edge of the village, in a meadow on a bluff overlooking the ocean, exposed on all sides. One of the oldest houses in Northeast Harbor, it was built in the style known as "New England farmhouse," although the man who built it in the 1860s, Sands Whitmore, was not a farmer but a sea captain. For me, it's an irresistible example of Maine vernacular architecture: white clapboard, green shutters, sharply peaked roofs and gables. It's not quite "big house, little house, back house, barn," but close. It has small rooms with fireplaces, old doors with latches, and painted wooden floors. Its rambling floor plan evolved over a hundred and forty-some years and we don't know for sure which rooms are original. Looking over the meadow where lupin and daisies bloom in spring, there's a small covered porch with nasturtiums spilling onto it. We added a deck on the sea side where we watch the sunsets—a structure and an activity that Captain Whitmore would no doubt have found frivolous in the extreme.

Not surprisingly, the village has gone through as many changes as the house since I was a child—more, in fact. But the Northeast Harbor in my mind's eye is always the one that was there in about 1945. My father was still an officer on a Naval ship, in Curaçao, a Dutch island off the coast of Venezuela, and my mother and Yan brought me and my younger brothers, Walter and Billy, up from Philadelphia on the Bar Harbor Express. I was nine, Walter six, Billy three. We hadn't been to Maine since before the war, and I barely remembered it. The overnight train ride was so exciting that for a while it eclipsed the anticipation of the August that lay ahead. Dinner in the dining car! Sleeping in an upper berth! Ringing for the unfortunate porter! until Yan put a stop to it. The phrase "Bar Harbor Express" is, for many in my generation, emotionally charged, and even writing the name evokes nostalgia.

We did not stay in Four Winds that year; my mother needed her own space, and three active young children at once were "too much for Muzzie's nerves," or so Yan said. Ahead of time, I had been told we were going to stay in a "cottage," which I was looking forward to. I knew what a cottage looked like from my fairy-tale books: one story, white, thatched roof, red door centered between two windows, chimney. When we arrived at a large, brown-shingled house surrounded by tall spruce trees which made it quite dark inside, I felt bitterly disappointed. I did not know yet that any building lived in by a summer person is, in local parlance, a "cottage," no matter what it looks like or how grand it might be.

So what was the village itself like in 1945? To be truthful, many of my memories of the '40s and '50s are jumbled together and I can't be entirely sure about just which buildings were where. In the last act of Thornton Wilder's *Our Town*, Emily Webb, who has died in childbirth, in her twenties, is allowed to come back from the land of the dead to visit her village, Grover's Corners. She chooses her twelfth birthday, and is astonished to see Main Street as it was then—there is so much she had forgotten. Being still living, I lack Emily's opportunity to see Northeast Harbor whole at a certain moment in time. All I can say is: this is how I remember our own Main Street the summer I was nine. This is not a history paper.

Gas was rationed, and there were few cars on the roads, and it did not occur to anyone to require their children to wear helmets while bicycling. I was allowed to ride my bike alone, all around the village. Walter bicycled too, but accompanied by my mother on her own bike, with a seat on the back for little Billy. With my new freedom came responsibilities: picking up both the mail at the Post Office, twice a day, and Muzzie's newspapers, at McGrath's Variety Store. Presiding over the counter was a Mrs. Bain with one arm permanently in a sling, I never knew why. I had been taught to say politely, "May I please have Mrs. Walter L. Foulke's *Bangor Daily News*?" which I did, religiously, every time, to the amusement of the big boys who hung around the store, and who would mock me, repeating my polite request in falsetto voices and guffawing, as I fled the yahoos on my bicycle. McGrath's, the beating heart of the village, is still where it was, and still run by the same family. The Post Office, too, stands in the same place, only now we have keys for our boxes instead of combination locks.

Where the Northeast Harbor branch of the Bar Harbor Bank stands now was the tantalizing Pastime Theater, whose movies changed every two or three days. Big, full-colored posters of Coming Attractions were out front, promising exciting movies about passionate love and war, which I was never allowed to see. I yearned over those posters. It was not until I was fourteen that I was liberated into the heady delights of the Pastime. Admission was fifty cents; children under twelve paid twenty-five. I don't remember any movies I saw—by the time I was allowed in, I was more interested in who was there with whom than in the movie itself. The Pastime burned in the 1960s, and I still feel wistful when I look at the Bar Harbor Bank. It's a superior bank, which sends us birthday cards signed by all who work in the Northeast Harbor branch—what other bank does that?—but it is not the Pastime.

Next to the Pastime was Brown's Taxi, long vanished, but essential during the years of gas rationing. Then came Mr. Stanley's Fish Market, now a gift shop. In 1945, you could catch flounder (delicious) and pollock (barely edible) from the Sea Street Dock. Old Mr. Stanley, the father of Mr. David Stanley, who succeeded him, would give a nickel apiece for the flounder I caught, if they were big enough. I suspect Muzzie had a hand in Mr. Stanley's willingness to take me on as a supplier. The smaller flounder, and the pollock, came home to be prepared by the grumpy cook. No cook in the kitchen now, and no fish in the harbor—not even the spiny scuplin, so ugly that I hated catching them and taking them off my hook. The harbor was dredged years ago to accommodate more and larger yachts, the Sea Street Dock grew into a marina, with long finger piers for sleek sailing and motor yachts. Most of the fishing boats retreated to Bass Harbor.

Stanley's Fish Market lasted a long time, nearly a hundred years; I miss its pungent smells and its utter basic-ness: in the front room, a roll-top desk with a spindle for sales slips, and a large black register for cash sales which gave a most satisfying ca-ching. In the back room were deep sinks and marble slabs for cleaning fish, an ice chest or two, and a lobster tank. Mr. David Stanley kept the records of what was ordered and what was charged in his head—accurately, according to my mother.

What else? There was Ellery Holmes's Store, which sold utilitarian clothing: yellow slickers—"sou'westers"— sneakers, rubber boots, and flannel shirts. There were several grocery stores where my mother and grandmother used their red and blue points for rationed items like meat and butter. The Pine Tree, the Hillcrest, Ober's were right on Main Street; the I.G.A. was up on Summit Street. It later turned into Small's Market, but eventually folded and transmogrified first, into an art gallery, and finally into a private house. The Pine Tree Market is the sole survivor, but always in peril, now that better roads make the big supermarkets in Bar Harbor and Ellsworth more accessible. Now, hard spirits and fine wines are a big part of the Pine Tree's business. In the 1940s, no alcohol was sold anywhere in Northeast Harbor—it was available only at the State Store in Bar Harbor. Near the Pine Tree was Mrs. Flye's lunch counter; when I was older, my friends and I would giggle over the notion of a lunch counter called Flye's.

Like the other kids, I was enamored of the drugstore's old-fashioned soda fountain and its vanilla milkshakes. That summer of 1945, I had my first and last banana split there, paid for with two weeks' allowance. It was a wonder: two halves of banana in an oblong dish, three scoops of ice cream in different flavors, a tower of whipped cream with a cherry on top. I can still remember how ill I felt afterwards from gorging.

I miss Walls's colorful little shop, selling bunches of flowers from his nursery, in glass jars. It's now a space for trunk shows. In kind Mrs. Tracy's Store, you could buy "dry goods" like needle and thread, yarn, and underwear; it's now a store which supplies miscellaneous items for decorating the summer cottages. I remember at least one antique store, P.P. Hill, which Muzzie patronized, and British Tweeds, selling cashmere sweaters and wool suits and capes, and wool plaid Bermuda shorts. (The weather was cooler in summer then—there's little need for British woolens now.) The Kimball Shop was a rich jumble of knick-knacks, dishes, toys, lamps, a far cry from the beautiful and well-organized household-goods store it has become. Miss Kimball was, to a nine-year-old, a terrifying mountain of a woman with frizzy red hair who did not want children fingering her merchandise and, when we ventured curiously in, scolded us out in short order.

Over the ensuing decades, the balance between "summer" and "winter" enterprises has shifted dramatically, and sometimes I think of the art galleries, real estate agencies, antique stores and clothing boutiques as like purple loosestrife, forcing out the indigenous plants. One evening recently, I complained grumpily to a fellow guest at a party that there were very few "authentic" places left in Northeast Harbor. "What do you mean by 'authentic'?" he asked, reasonably enough. I laughed and said sheepishly, " 'Authentic' means it was there when I was a child." Unreasonable, but true for me.

Back to when I was nine. My bicycle freedom extended to more than Main Street. Weekday mornings, I biked to rowing class at the Northeast Harbor Fleet headquarters at Gilpatrick Cove, which I don't think has changed much since the 1940s, although the simple "Clubhouse" has been enlarged. Sometimes we rowers were taken sailing in Bullseyes by the instructors, glamorous older boys sixteen and seventeen. One of them used to tease me and say, "You're my girlfriend, Louisa, aren't you?" I would blush and shake my head; I doubt if he knew it, but he made my heart beat faster and I wanted him to mean what he said. (This man is now well over eighty. He and his wife have joined the growing ranks of "year round summer people" in Northeast Harbor. I have never told him my secret, and never will.) After rowing class, my friends and I went to the swimming pool, which was only a fenced-off semi-circle of murky green and frigid ocean, slightly sun-warmed. In the little entrance hall, supervised by the dignified, bespectacled Miss Wood wearing ankle-length dresses, was a chalk board telling you the day's water temperature, which was usually in the high sixties or low seventies. If the tide was high enough, you could make the pool feel warmer by going into the ocean first. There are today many women my age, loyal to the spirit of those hardy days, who still swim *only* in the original pool and the ocean, eschewing entirely the standard turquoise blue, heated rectangle added some fifty years back, maybe sixty, and known to our generation as "the new pool." On rainy days, there was the library with its open wood-burning fireplace, and a wealth of books to choose from.

What else did we do? Most of life was family-centered. In the evening, the grown-ups sometimes gathered at each other's houses for a drink, or small dinners for six or eight prepared by the cook brought from Philadelphia for the summer, but there were no catered parties. (No decorators, either; the prevailing style could be termed "eclectic summer cottage shabby." Summer cottages were sold furnished.) We didn't go many places in the car, because of gas rationing. We did take the mail boats to the Cranberry Islands, for picnics, and to the church fairs. I remember the potato races and the three-legged races, and the fish chowder prepared by the ladies of the altar guild. There were beautiful patchwork quilts for sale, made over the long winter.

Like most people we knew, we went to St. Mary's-by-the-Sea Episcopal Church on Sunday, and to the brief Sunset Service on Sunday evening, on the lawn of what was then the Cromwell estate, overlooking Somes Sound. We children and the younger grown-ups sat on the grass, older folks sat on folding chairs. Miss Pendle-ton, the church choir mistress, played the portable organ, furiously pumping the foot pedals, to accompany the rag-ged hymn-singing. A member of the congregation gave a brief homily. No one had to wear church clothes to Sunset Service and the whole thing was over in half an hour, so we children did not object to this second Sunday obser-vance. Sunset service exists now pretty much as it did, an island of continuity.

One hymn we always sang, the summer of 1945, was "Eternal Father, Strong to Save," the verses for the Army and Air Force as well as for the Navy. The verse about "those in peril on the sea" still makes me well up. Half consciously, I did absorb the reality that 1945 was, for the adults, an extremely anxious time, waiting for the War to end, hoping fervently for the safe return of the men and boys not already dead. It never occurred to me that my father could die, but I missed him.

On VJ Day, joyful celebration broke out. The fire engine gave rides to Bar Harbor and back for all who could scramble on board. My mother considered me too young for this excitement, and I did not go, except in my imagination. I was consoled by the knowledge that now my father would be able to come home, which he did, within a few months.

I acknowledge that there is a classic tendency to look back at earlier eras through a "dome of many-colored glass," and yet I do believe that even for grown-ups, life really *was* simpler then on Mt. Desert, and stayed simple for at least another ten years: simpler than in the glory days of Bar Harbor and the lavish parties of the 1920s, and simpler than now when the locus of fashion in the Second Gilded Age has shifted to Northeast Harbor. In retrospect, I lived in a golden age between two gilded ones.

The golden age is long over. Bill and I are now members of the oldest generation, facing changes in ourselves as well as in the village. There's no buffer between us and mortality any more. I will never again meet old ladies on Main Street who hail me by my mother's maiden name (Louisa Wood), as I did when my grandparents were still alive. However, much remains.

We have considered establishing ourselves elsewhere in Maine in summer. We could find in other corners of the coast all the dear clichés: the cry of gulls, the chugging of lobster boats starting up at dawn, the mournful clang of bell buoys, and the sound of unseen oars rhythmically splashing in the fog. But we are tied here by love:

for a brother and his family next door; another brother and his, four miles away, a sister fifteen minutes from our house and all their children and grandchildren visiting throughout the summer. And love of this specific spot, of the hills we call mountains, the parade of sailboats scudding in and out of Somes Sound, the little bridge over Gilpatrick Cove. McGrath's! We are condemned to stay.

There are worse fates.

MUZZIE

M y father's mother, whom I called "Muzzie," was a short, compact, excitable woman with strong, persuasive powers. In his old age, my father enjoyed telling the story of how she met Nelson, her second husband, in February 1924. Dad's older sister Anita, then fifteen, was at boarding school in Connecticut. Muzzie was on a cruise in the Caribbean when she got a wire from the school saying that Anita had been hospitalized for an emergency appendectomy. Muzzie, frantic, cornered the captain, fixed him with her expressive brown eyes full of tears, and implored him to turn back as far as Cuba where she could disembark and take another boat to Miami. He was helpless before her. She refused to go away until he gave in. Dad used to laugh, imagining the consternation of the other passengers at the change of itinerary, which of course took place. The passengers may have disembarked and enjoyed a few hours in Havana, but the story does not include that part; we just have to imagine it.

From Miami, Muzzie was able to telephone the school. Anita was doing fine, but would have to stay in the hospital for two weeks, not unusual in that era. Muzzie, convinced Anita needed a warm climate for her convalescence, wanted her to come to Florida as soon as she was released. But where? She was not much taken by Miami but had a good friend who wintered in Palm Beach, so she went there and looked for a house to rent.

The real estate agent who took her around was Nelson Odman, a handsome, charming, Nordic blond Swede eleven years younger. Muzzie was forty-three, six years into a comfortable but lonely widowhood. They were instantly attracted to each other, although they had different goals. Muzzie wanted love and marriage, Nelson wanted a life of ease, although that was not at first apparent to her. By the time she and Nelson married, a year later, Muzzie had begun saying that he was really nine years younger, an age difference which sounded more appropriate and in which she came to believe. The most sensible of her older brothers, Ario Pardee, recognized a fortune hunter when he saw one, and insisted on what the French call a "séparation de biens": Nelson was not to inherit any of her assets. Daddy used to muse that his life and that of his siblings would have been very different indeed without Ario's perspicacity. I don't know how much this limitation bothered Nelson. Muzzie's money enabled him to live very well in the present, and this may have been more important to him than the future.

For their winters, the newlyweds built a beautiful Italianate palazzo on the shores of Lake Worth which they called "La Torra Bianca." I knew no Italian or Spanish, and I guess no one else in the family did either, because when I was in college and wrote a story about this house, a linguistically inclined classmate pointed out that if the name had been truly Italian, it would have been " Il Torre Bianco" and in Spanish it would have been "La Torra Blanca." The architectural style, and the antiques Muzzie and Nelson furnished it with, were distinctly Italian. On their honeymoon, they had gone on an extended buying trip in Europe and brought back a large number of exquisite period credenzas, chairs, chests, gaming tables, sideboards, daybeds, many still trickling down through the Foulke generations. Whatever Nelson did not have (integrity, loyalty, money of his own—he retired early from the real estate business) he did have excellent taste. Marrying a committed shopper with deep pockets must have been a dream come true for him. When Muzzie died, my parents gave me some of her jewelry, including a diamond watch Nelson had given her as a wedding present. "If he gave it to her, I don't think I want it" I said. "Don't worry," said my father. "She paid the bill for it."

MUZZIE'S FIRST HUSBAND, Walter Foulke, died of pneumonia at the start of the 1918 influenza epidemic, in an army camp in San Antonio, Texas. Muzzie was left an attractive widow of thirty-five with three children: Pardee, eleven; Anita, nine; and Billy—my father—just five. Walter Foulke came from a Philadelphia Quaker family. His father had been a teacher, then a lawyer; Walter himself had been a revered football star at Princeton in an era when that connoted "character" and "discipline." After his marriage, he went into business and became a solid citizen, a loving husband, and a devoted father. Nothing in her life with him, or in her protected childhood, had equipped Muzzie with the requisite defenses against an operator like Nelson.

Ultimately, Nelson's flagrant multiple infidelities became too much for Muzzie to bear. She initiated a separation, and then a divorce. Although my parents withheld from me the details of both the marriage and the divorce, my father used to say occasionally, his voice heavy with the unspoken, thinking of Nelson's Nordic blond hair, "Not all villains are dark." (Dad did let slip, in an unguarded moment when he was in his nineties, that Nelson slept with the maids, among others. Classic, and humiliating.) To their dying days, my parents told me almost nothing about Nelson. I had always loved to write, and they were afraid I would grow up to be a real writer and publish embarrassing family stories. So there is much that I do not know.

After the divorce, she took back Foulke as her last name. I knew nothing of Nelson until I was about eight and, in a closet in her Palm Beach house, I found a coat hanger labeled "Mrs. Odman." "Who's Mrs. Odman?" I asked Yan. "Your grandmother's second husband," she said. "They were divorced the year after you were born and she went back to being Mrs. Foulke." She would say nothing else. I was not quite sure what "divorced" meant, but sensed that it was a taboo subject. I was her first grandchild, and her favorite, born during the divorce, when she was miserable. According to my parents, my arrival, and the hope for a happier future it represented, helped pull her through a period of bitterness and pain. She doted on me and I loved her back, dearly.

My father was twelve when his mother and Nelson were married. Many years later, before the wedding of his older brother Pardee to a divorced woman with a twelve-year-old daughter, Dad said to me, "Be especially nice to Patsy. It's no fun to go to your own mother's wedding." He always said, though, that Nelson had not been unkind to him, or to Pardee and Anita, but treated them distantly, never trying to be a stepfather. Dad always claimed he had been saved, not long after the wedding, by joining Pardee at St. Paul's School; he was grateful all his life for the male role models he had there.

Muzzie kept La Torra Bianca for several years after the divorce. She loved Palm Beach and what she saw as its glamour. She had spent her early childhood in Hazelton, Pennsylvania, a coal mining town where she was the daughter of the hated and feared mine owners, the Pardees. She was the youngest of nine children, one of whom died at the age of five, ten days before Muzzie's

birth in 1882. Her father moved the family to Germantown, a neighborhood in Philadelphia, when she was still
very young. My father wrote, in a self-published biogra-
phy of his grandfather:

"Sometime during the early eighties, Grandfather
began to grow dissatisfied with living in Hazelton.
Devoted as he was to his father and his whole family,
he thought the place too small and confining for his
children. He and Grandmother came to the conclu-
sion that their children would benefit by going to
school and making friends with contemporaries who
came from a world where the very name of Hazelton
meant nothing, and where the Pardees were not
important people. Since he had relinquished his position as manager of his father's mines, Grandfather
had no further obligations on that score..."[1]

MY FATHER, ALWAYS, had a knack for putting things
into a positive light. No mention in his book, for example,
of the Lattimer Massacre of 1897, when Pardee manage-
ment deputies fired on unarmed striking Polish and Slovak
miners, killing 19 and wounding 49; or of the 1972 Buffalo
Creek Disaster in 1972, caused by the Pittston Coal Company operating on Pardee land. Books have been written
about these incidents, and for a while, my brother Walter
had them in a row on what he called the Disaster Shelf.

1. *Calvin Pardee,*1841-1923: *His Family and his Enterprises.* C. Pardee Foulke
and William G. Foulke, 1979

Even though Muzzie did not live long in Hazelton, she accompanied her family on visits back there, and I have always felt that the shadow of the place and its mines haunted her. She and Walter Foulke lived in a substantial but modest whitewashed house called Mill House, in Whitemarsh, just outside the northwestern Philadelphia suburbs. Quaker that he was, my grandfather liked living "simply," a relative term to be sure, but he eschewed luxury. After his death, Muzzie let loose her own tastes. She sought out places where people lived, ate, and dressed well, where houses and gardens were elegant and well-tended, places like Nice, Cannes, and Paris, places where people gave and went to parties and generally had a good time— all of them antitheses of Hazelton and its coal dust. She did not drink alcohol herself but enjoyed the company of those who did, especially when they were drinking champagne. I don't think she read F. Scott Fitzgerald, but if she had, she would have recognized much of her life. Palm Beach in the 1920s suited her. I have a portrait of her painted in 1927. She has dark brown hair, fashionably arranged, and wistful eyes. She wears a long string of pearls and a sable stole my father says was borrowed for the occasion. By the time I was aware of her, she was a plump, gray-haired woman in her late fifties (to me, very old) with lots of freckles and a large, soft, comforting bosom. Her eyes were still as they are in the portrait, reflecting a sadness behind the smile. She loved to laugh and when she was really amused, she literally laughed until she cried, wiping her eyes with one of her embroidered linen handkerchiefs.

Although I visited Muzzie in the Palm Beach houses she owned subsequent to La Torre Bianca, and in Four Winds in Maine, and went often to Mill House in Whitemarsh, when I picture her, I see her in La Torra Bianca. I remember the house well, even though I must have been only eight or nine when Muzzie sold it. It was on Banyan Road, and the banyans themselves were fascinating to me, with their gnarled and sprawling roots and branches, making me think of trees in illustrated fairy tales, Maeterlink's "The Bluebird" in particular. To me, the house was a fairy-tale palace, with its circular staircase winding up into a square tower, even though that led only to a little-used sitting room. A curved, marble staircase with a wrought iron railing went up from the front hall to the second floor. The spacious, high-ceilinged living room and French doors along one side, opened onto a flowery terrace, and beyond that, was a walled garden full of lemon and fragrant mock-orange trees. On the terrace was a huge aviary filled with bright tropical birds , which I used to watch for hours on end. There were two separate cages inside the house, one for Bulbul and the other for Troupiole; they did not get along with the aviary birds or with each other. Bulbul had a nasty temper and would bite if you put a finger in his cage, as I quickly discovered. "He won't bite on Thursdays," said Mossa, the Norwegian maid, but I never tested this theory. (Thursday was Mossa's day out.)

I was accompanied on these Florida visits by my devoted Yan. We would take the overnight train from

Philadelphia, and I looked forward to the trips even more than the visits. I would be so wild with anticipation that Yan and Mum took to not telling me about the trip until the last minute. Usually, Yan and I would board the Floridian, a noble dragon which came puffing majestically into Thirtieth Street Station from someplace north, while we waited on the platform until the train stopped and the porter helped us aboard. In each Pullman car there were regular seats which were transformed at night into sleeping spaces, upper and lower berths, and some private bedrooms, called "drawing rooms." Yan and I would share one of these, with a wide sitting bench which turned into a bed at night and an upper berth hidden away in the wall. We went to the dining car for meals on tables with white tablecloths and a menu with many adjectives. (Peas, for example were "fresh green garden peas.") While we were at dinner, a porter would go to our bedroom, make up the bench as a bed and pull down the upper berth, which was mine. At one end of each Pullman car there was a "dressing room" for ladies where there was room to change, equipped with tables and mirrors for applying make up. At the other end was a smoker for gentlemen. The cigar smoke I could smell when I went past it made me feel ill.

I remember one trip when Walter was along too—he was perhaps three at the time—and two of Muzzie's miniature schnauzers, Iris and Koolie. When the train stopped, Yan would get out to walk the dogs, and I would be terrified that she would not get back on the train before it started to move again. After one stop, Yan did not come back to our drawing room for what seemed like hours and I was sure she had been left behind. I wondered, with rising panic, what Walter and I would do by ourselves. Then she showed up and explained she'd just been having a conversation about the schnauzers with a dog-loving fellow-passenger.

I had been an adult a long time before I realized that it must have been a considerable sacrifice for my mother to let Yan go with me to Florida for a month at a time, leaving her to cope with my two rambunctious younger brothers. Muzzie was devoted to Yan and enjoyed her company, but even if she hadn't been, it would not have occurred to Muzzie to take care of me herself. For people of means, it was an age of servants. In addition to Mossa, there was her husband Egel, the butler; a little-seen cook in the recesses of a kitchen where I was not permitted to enter; and a cheerful black laundress named Hattie who came in by the day. My father remembers Hattie saying dreamily, "June is such a nice month. I always pick June for my weddin's." There was also a chauffeur, Reynolds, who drove the Packard. He was the brother of Anna Rowntree, my father's old nurse, still retained by Muzzie to do light housework. My father told me that Reynolds had been shell-shocked in World War I. When we were being driven places, I stared at the criss-cross pattern of wrinkles on the back of Reynolds's neck and wonder how it got that way, and wondered if it had to do with shell shock. When Muzzie and her friends went shopping on Worth Avenue, Reynolds and the other chauffeurs would wait patiently for their employers, and I remember thinking what a terrible job it must be to spend so much time waiting for someone.

There was a routine. Once we had finished our breakfast, Yan and I would come into Muzzie's room to say good morning. She always had breakfast in bed surrounded by dogs, and when I opened the door, they would move closer to her and yap noisily until they were placated with tidbits from her tray. They were very jealous of me or of anyone they perceived as rivals for Muzzie's attention.

After Muzzie had made her telephone calls, Reynolds would drive us all to the Bath and Tennis Club, where there was a stretch of beach, a dining room where a buffet lunch was served every day, and a vast salt-water pool where I had swimming and diving lessons from patient Mr. Gardello, a deeply tanned man with an Italian accent. Yan told me I had learned to swim from him when I was three, although I don't remember that process. After my swimming lesson, the great treat was a peeled orange on a stick which I could have only when in a bathing suit and near the ocean's edge as the delicious sticky juice would get all over me.

A couple of moments stand out. Once, there was a party next door at which the Duke and Duchess of Windsor were guests. Muzzie was invited, and Yan held me up so that I could see the Duke over the wall. Yan, like so many other British citizens, had a special affection for him, even though she deplored his marriage and still mourned over his abdication in 1936. And once, I had a birthday party in the garden when I was five or six and discovered pinwheels. I ran around showing other children that if you ran, the pinwheel would go around and around. I know from a photograph that Walter was there on that occasion, and perhaps my parents, too. There are a dozen children in two rows, mostly girls, all in white, and wearing white shoes and socks. All but one or two of them look pretty glum, including me. Walter, wearing a white shirt and shorts, is scowling and holding a battered doll named Poppa that he was fond of. My parents and brothers must have come to Palm Beach some of the time. But the only visits I remember are those when Yan and I were there by ourselves and those when I went alone, after Yan had left the family. Muzzie claimed that having the energetic boys around was too much for her.

WE WERE IN Cape May when I learned that Muzzie had sold La Torra Bianca and was "building a new house," so I must have been around seven or eight, as we came back to Chestnut Hill when I was nine. I don't recall being upset by the news but I was astonished to hear Muzzie was building a house. I pictured her on her knees with bricks and a trowel and was tremendously impressed. It was several days before someone straightened me out on this. The new house was called "Pink House" and although I remember vaguely what it looked like, I don't have sharp visual memories of it. I remember the lush, tropical smell of the garden, so welcome when I arrived from winter, and a doll house in which a large spider took up residence for a few memorable hours. I also remember a well-stocked F.A.O. Schwarz toy store on a nearby corner into whose windows I would stare longingly. I desperately wanted a gorgeously dressed and fiercely expensive bride doll, and Muzzie, who wanted to give me everything I expressed interest in, would have been happy to buy it on the spot, but Yan intervened. "There has to be a limit," she said firmly. "Louisa has plenty of dolls." She did not approve of Muzzie's spoiling me and did what she could to keep it under control, with only partial success. Yan tried to drum into me that I could not have everything I wanted, but Muzzie's message was quite the opposite.

When I was between ten and twelve, either there were winters when I did not go to Palm Beach, or else they have all blurred together. I have distinct and painful memories of my last two visits, both of which were to yet a third Palm Beach house, this one next to the golf course. The first of these visits was during spring vacation, when I was thirteen and in the ninth grade at Springside School. Adolescence changed everything, as it tends to. Two years earlier, Yan had gone to work for the Prizer family; now that Billy was in school all day, Mum did not need her. I was on my own. Muzzie wanted to ensure that I had a good time, and she knew that for teenagers, that meant the opportunity to have a social life with others the same age. She arranged for me to be in a tennis tournament and to go to a dance at the Everglades Club, and a dinner before it that someone she knew had organized. "You need to meet some young people," she said.

I became acutely aware that there was an in-group of people my age who had known each other for years. Most lived in Palm Beach year round. Both tennis tournament and dance were exercises in humiliation for me. Although I was a pretty good tennis player by the standards of the Chestnut Hill Cricket Club, I was no match for the girls my age who lived in Palm Beach and played tennis all year round—I was out at the end of the first round. They all went to Palm Beach Private (it was the one private school, and that was its name), or so it appeared, and knew each other. They wore lipstick, had beautiful tans, and ran around the courts in swingy pleated tennis skirts, making me feel small and unsophisticated in my camp shorts.

The dinner before the dance wasn't bad, as I ran into Lois Upham, a girl I had known long ago in Cape May, New Jersey, and who didn't know anyone either. Her father, who had run the summer theater in Cape May, had decided to try his luck with a winter one in Palm Beach. No one danced with me, despite the new long, pink tulle dress Muzzie had bought for me, but no one danced with Lois either, and at least we had each other. It was Lois who noticed before anyone else did that my period had come upon me unexpectedly and that a red stain was spreading on the back of my dress. She walked behind me to the ladies' room, helped wash out the stain as best we could, and I stood by while she called Muzzie and asked her to come and get me.

Tennis and dances were clearly not going to be successes, and I felt I had to at least go back to Springside after vacation with a tan. To this end, I sunbathed for several hours nonstop beside the Bath and Tennis Club pool. No hat, no sun lotion (sunscreens like those we have now did not exist.) By the next day, my face was swollen and purple, and I was running a high fever. Muzzie clucked over me and called a doctor. "Sun poisoning," he said. "You should have known better." I *did* know better, in fact, and probably half-consciously had wanted time out from being an outsider pretending for Muzzie's sake to have a good time. The doctor said to stay indoors in a dark room with cold compresses on my eyes, and I was happy to do so. Nice Lois came to see me a couple of times, and Muzzie was pleased that I had a friend. By the time I went back to Chestnut Hill, the swelling had gone down but I had no tan—only pink, peeling skin.

The following year, I went down during the spring vacation of my first year at Farmington. This went a little better. There were a few Farmington girls who were also in Palm Beach, not close friends, but people who smiled and said hello, and let me hang out around the pool with them. The Palm Beach Private crowd had gone off to different boarding schools, and although they were home for vacation, they were not as close knit or tanned as formerly. Again, there was an Everglades Club dance—no Lois, probably her father's theater hopes hadn't panned out—but this time, a few boys danced with me, including the older brother of one of the Farmington girls who asked to take me home afterwards. He took me first to a night club and ordered Tom Collinses for us both, which I thought extremely daring. Something to brag about when I was back in school.

This was the last vacation I ever spent in Palm Beach. Muzzie became very sick in the late spring with a perforated ulcer. Dad told me that Nelson discovered this and began writing to her. She was thrilled that he had gotten in touch, and answered his letters. "He's after money," said Dad gloomily. "I think she still loves him." She may have given him some before her death. But he did not inherit.

She died in the Chestnut Hill Hospital on June 20, 1951, of complications from the ulcer surgery, including phlebitis. She was sixty-nine, but pretending to the last to be two years younger; she gave her birth date to the hospital as 1884. Mum and Dad, when they told me she had just died, asked if I wanted to see her, and I went to her hospital room where I had visited several times. The door was closed. I opened it and saw an unrecognizable old woman, eyes closed but mouth still open, all life drained from her face, her skin yellowing. This body in no way resembled the Muzzie I had known, and I went away quite shaken. It was the first time I had seen anyone dead. She was buried in the graveyard of St. Thomas's Church, Whitemarsh, beside her first husband Walter Foulke.

She left a strange will. To each of her three children she left a third of her estate, but my Uncle Pardee's share was left in trust: he was to get the income during his lifetime, but if he died without issue and Anita died before him—which is exactly what happened—the principal would all come to me. Nothing to my brothers, very unfairly. It is a great tribute to them that we have always been on good terms. Luckily, they have done well for themselves; nevertheless, buried resentment pops out occasionally. What was she thinking of? That women had a harder time than men making money of their own? Or was it just flat out, shocking, favoritism?

Had Muzzie lived longer, we might not have continued to enjoy a close relationship. In adolescence, I began to notice her faults. She had no education beyond finishing school and her outlook was limited, her reactions frequently irrational. When I turned twelve, I began to notice her anti-Semitism and be distressed by it. I had been influenced by a novel called *Gentleman's Agreement*, one of the first contemporary novels for adults I read, and I hated to hear Muzzie rail against the Jews who were moving into Palm Beach. I tried to argue with her, but this led nowhere. She could be ungenerous; I remember her becoming extremely agitated by the request of a blind friend to accompany her to church on Easter. "I don't want to walk down the aisle with that dog!" she kept saying. Much later, I began to realize how difficult she had made my mother's life; having Muzzie as a mother-in-law must have required vast reserves of patience and forbearance.

To me, however, she was consistently a warm, loving, and uncritical presence, and I think of her still, warts and all, with enormous affection for this complex, fallible human being—lucky and unlucky, generous and ungenerous, and laughing until the tears came.

PART II

YOUTH

DANCES

D ances! The word suggests gaiety and fun. Yet even at their best, dances aroused in me a measure of terror. The first dances I went to (tap lessons in Cape May didn't count) were the Friday afternoon dancing classes at the Philadelphia Cricket Club, when I was in the fifth and sixth grades at Miss Zara's. They were once a month during the school year. The children who attended these went to single-sex schools, and the classes provided structured opportunities to mingle coeducationally. We "danced," after a fashion, to music on black 78 rpm records on a Victrola. Girls wore party dresses, white socks, and patent-leather Mary Janes. Boys wore jackets and ties, and white gloves. I had only one party dress, my frugal mother and Yan thinking it an unnecessary extravagance to have more, since I was growing so fast. It was peach-colored and the short sleeves were filmy and translucent. We used to change into our party dresses at school and go directly to the Cricket Club, and I remember the embarrassment I felt the first time I wore this dress when I realized that the sleeves of my undershirt were highly visible through the peach organza. My classmates teased me and I would have given anything to go home instead of to the dancing class. But I went, and resolved to make sure that next time I wore a sleeveless undershirt.

At these dancing classes, so significant to the girls and so reluctantly attended by the boys, the two teachers were both women who would dance together to demonstrate the dances they hoped to teach us: box step, foxtrot, waltz. They changed the black records to match the lesson. They would pair the boys and girls up in different ways—by birthday month, for example, or by asking the girls to put their bracelets in a hat and the boys to fish them out and dance with the owners. Sometimes at the end of the class there was a "ladies' choice" and sometimes a boys'. I was too shy to ask anyone I admired to dance, and I did not admire those who asked me. One time, I had an eye infection and had to wear a patch over one eye for a week, including the day of the Halloween dancing class. Yan, to help make up for the patch, took me to Van Horne's costume rental, where I chose a magnificent gypsy costume. It didn't help much. People noticed the eye patch, not the lovely red velvet and the jingly beads. "Are you a pirate?" someone asked.

These were not dances at their best. They were alleviated, however, by the Mexican Hat Dance, the Conga Line, and the Bunny Hop, none of which required either grace or conversation.

In the seventh grade, I was excluded from the next series of dances, the Friday Evenings, because I was not yet twelve; these dances were organized by age, not grade in school. Although my mother pleaded on my behalf with the director, and even took me to see her to demonstrate how mature I was (a visit that was probably counterproductive), she was adamant. At home, I cried and complained, and my father said for heaven's sake he couldn't understand why there was all this fuss over a dancing class that, when he was a boy, he had done his level best to escape, going out on the terrace of the Cricket Club to avoid being made to dance. I began to realize how deep and wide the gender gap could be.

The "Friday Evening" assumed an importance far out of proportion with its frequency. Each one provided enough food for school gossip for the intervening weeks: who had danced with whom, who "liked" whom ("I know he likes you." "Are you sure? How do you know?" "He told Molly he did"—and so on.)

One classmate, Edith Baird, was also shut out for being under age. On the Friday evenings of the dances, she and I would have supper together, either at her house or at mine, and amuse ourselves with a game afterwards. Neither of our families had television, which was still a new thing. Sometimes a parent would take us to a movie, and once Mr. Baird took us to see Martha Graham's modern dance company. Edith and I were fascinated. We had seen ballet, but never anything so avant-garde. Mr. Baird shocked me by going right to sleep and snoozing throughout, just like men in the cartoons about opera I'd seen in *The New Yorker.*

Edith and I got on well, but we were small consolation for each other. We imagined all the flirtations and incipient romances that must be happening to everyone else. We knew that we would spend the next weeks hungrily picking up crumbs of gossip from the more fortunate. We survived and were initiated the following year into desideratum of the Friday Evenings for our eighth grade year. Curiously, I remember the pain of being left out in seventh grade, but almost nothing about the ones I actually went to in the eighth.

With one exception: I can still see Cussy (for Cuthbert) Swope and Peggy Bogan, already a pair, jitterbugging so energetically and well that everyone else would stop dancing and form a circle around them to gaze in awe. Later, when she was sixteen, Peggy scandalized us all by becoming pregnant; her parents and Cussy's obliged them to marry and withdraw from school, so that Peggy could look after the baby and Cussy could work to support them all. But that was still ahead, and at their jitterbugging zenith, anyone would have envied them.

Starting in my tenth grade year, I went to the Saturday Evening, officially called "dances," not "dancing classes." Luckily for me, admission was now by grade in school, not age. There were fewer of these, maybe three, at Christmas, Easter, June. They took place in the Barclay Hotel ballroom, downtown, which made them seem extremely grown up, though there was no alcohol. There was a real six-piece band, playing danceable show tunes and Cole Porter favorites, and the dress was formal for both boys and girls. The tempo was the Society Bounce, a term I hadn't heard then. There were a lot of new faces, girls and boys from the Main Line as well as my old Chestnut Hill buddies. By this time, I was in my first year at Farmington and I associate the joy of my first vacation home, at Christmas, with the excitement of my first Saturday Evening.

This was in 1950. The twist and rock and roll were a decade off, and boys and girls still danced holding on to each other; I often thought when my own children were growing up what a shame it was that they had missed the tactile experiences of dancing.

At these dances, there were, by design, many more boys than girls; there was a big stag line from which a boy would emerge and "cut in," sending the cuttee to look for someone else's shoulder to tap. A "popular" girl would dance for only a few minutes with a boy before being claimed by another. The more boys cut in, the more popular you looked, and the more popular you *became*, at least for the evening.

At that first Saturday Evening, I had on a red tulle dress which could have been strapless if my mother had allowed it to be. It came with little separate sleeves which were intended to be worn decoratively on the arms, but Mum had sewed them firmly to the bodice so that it would not look as though her fourteen-year-old daughter were wearing a strapless dress. Whether it was my almost-strapless red dress or a quirk of fate, I was much cut in on that evening, and one of the boys who kept coming back was a boy I had not met before named Jim. He, too, went to a New England boarding school, Brooks, and was two years older. I thought he was the handsomest boy I had ever seen—tall with dark brown hair and big dark brown eyes. He had broken a vertebra in his neck playing football and wore a white neck-brace and a white silk ascot instead of a shirt and black bow tie, and this, to me, enhanced his glamour. He was smitten with me and I with him.

Jim had his driver's license, which made him practically an adult. I was allowed to drive with him because my parents knew his parents. During that magical Christmas vacation, we went to parties together and to movies with another couple; my parents insisted on the second couple. We went to a New Year's Eve party together, and he kissed me at midnight. He invited me to come to the winter dance weekend at Brooks in February, and I accepted. I could hardly wait for it. Once back at our respective boarding schools, we exchanged letters several times a week; I lived for them.

Inevitably, heartbreak ensued. At the much-anticipated Brooks dance weekend, for reasons I never understood (and he probably didn't either), Jim fell out of love with me.

Maybe I didn't look the way he remembered me. Maybe the falling-out had begun earlier. Maybe I had answered his letters too eagerly. At any rate, he announced while we were on the dance floor that we were "too young to be so deeply involved." Entirely reasonable, and I could only numbly agree, but felt a tightness in my chest and a despair which did not dissipate for many months. During spring vacation, he fell in love with another girl named Kathy, prettier and dumber than I, and became even more involved with her than he had been with me. My heart developed another crack.

The culmination of this carefully choreographed progression of subscription dances was Coming Out, a term which my parents and their circle preferred to "making a début," which they found pretentious. Illogically, they were okay with "debutante party." (Since "coming out" has entirely changed its primary meaning, today my parents would probably go for "making a début" after all.) The custom was this: during the year following a girl's graduation from secondary school, almost always a private school, her family, parents or grandparents, gave her a formal dance. Such a dance's original purpose, starting in the 19th century, had been to present the young woman to "society" and let society know that she was ready for marriage to a suitable young man.

That none of us, neither young women nor young men, was anywhere near ready for marriage was beside the point. Up until the era when girls began going to college, these dances took place throughout the year, but by the 1950s they were crammed into the month of June, a couple of weeks in early September, the long Thanksgiving weekend, and Christmas vacation. Coming Out was a coming-of-age ritual which an anthropologist would identify as the induction into the tribe, which in my case was the relatively small group of old Philadelphians with tribal affinities to other east coast families in New York and Boston. Only the closest friends of the parent-hosts were invited—the emphasis was on the young people. Those of us who had been to boarding school went to parties in other cities as well as in our own, but here, I am focusing on Philadelphia coming out parties as they were, for me, at midcentury.

These events took place all over the Main Line suburbs and exurbs as well as in Chestnut Hill. Their size and extravagance varied. Some were in hotel ball rooms, some were in clubs, a few in private houses with living rooms big enough for dancing, and, in June and September, many were under large tents with dance floors, set up on the host's lawn. Under the surface, there was an ongoing unacknowledged but fierce competition that everyone was much too well bred to mention. A spacious dance floor was expected, as was good food, good music, and good champagne, but a party should not be too showy or have any taint of nouveau riche. The Meyer Davis Orchestra was considered the best; you paid a premium for getting Meyer Davis himself to conduct. My parents chose Mark Davis, a much less expensive bandleader capitalizing on the similarity of his name to the illustrious Meyer's.

Some parties were dinner-dances, but most were only dances, as they were less expensive. The mother of the debutante would suggest to her closest friends, whose daughters would be among the guests, that they give little dinners beforehand, so that the young people would have a chance to get to know each other and warm up for the main event. At these dinners, we got to practice small talk and the art of "turning the tables"—making sure you talked to both your dinner partners for a decent length of time, even if one was clearly cuter or easier to talk to than the other.

If no one going to the same dinner had offered me a ride, my parents would drop me at the dinner and expect me to find a way to get to from there to the dance. I was always terrified that no one would offer me a ride and that I would have to cadge one, which sometimes happened. They also expected me to find a ride home from the dance afterwards, although they always said I could call them if I needed one. They didn't suggest taxis, which were in short supply in the Philadelphia suburbs. I continue to be astonished by their position, which was not typical of my normally careful mother and father. They undoubtedly did not know how drunk many of the boys would get, and I never told them. The drinking laws were far less stringent than they are today and not enforced at private parties. These were the days when girls, most of whom stayed sober, felt it might humiliate a boy to demand his keys and take over the wheel, something that would spook him and all his friends. In the name of popularity and appeasement, we put our young lives at risk over and over.

By the time I was a senior at Farmington, I had read enough satire, fiction, and history to question the validity of coming out, which was designed to perpetuate a class system I had decided I did not believe in. I announced to my parents, who believed deeply in the importance of coming out, and in the significance of class, that I did not want a coming out party. "Fine," said my smart mother. "But then you can't go to everyone else's party either. It is not fair to accept that kind of hospitality when you are not prepared to offer it back." She had me. I was seventeen and the prospect of giving up all the parties that my friends were going to give, and go to, and talk non-stop about, not to mention all the pretty new dresses, was too much for me. I surrendered my principles with embarrassing speed.

The June after my graduation from Farmington, my parents and my grandmother Wood, Danny, gave me a dance for about a hundred and fifty, at Red Roof, her country house in Wawa. (Grandpa died when I was twelve.) Danny gave a dinner for thirty before it. My mother enlisted the aid of Mrs. Thompson, a widow who had fallen on impecunious times, but who understood the nuances of the rituals, and had developed a career as the milieu's trusted party-organizer. She had a master calendar and knew when each of the parties was scheduled, so that mothers could pick a date not in conflict with some other, possibly more prestigious, party. (I say "mothers" advisedly, as fathers were rarely involved in the details, as with weddings.) Mrs. Thompson and my mother made sure that other pre-dance dinners would be given, so that all the guests not coming to mine were invited somewhere and would not have to show up "cold" at ten o'clock for the dance. This required a certain amount of polite arm-twisting on my mother's part, but it was understood that later in the season, she and my father would do likewise for others: you give a dinner before my daughter's dance, and I'll give one before your daughter's.

Mrs. Thompson saw that the list of boys was triple the list of girls, so that there would be a long stag line and constant cutting in. These boys ranged in age from about eighteen to twenty-one or two—young men went to these parties for several years while girls had only one "season," although they might be invited to a few balls given by cousins or sisters the next year. For those giving big parties who didn't already know many boys, Mrs. Thompson had a List of recommended young men from nice families that she could vouch for as acceptable. A long stag line was key to the success of a dance, and it would have taken a felony to get a boy crossed off Mrs. Thompson's list if he had gone to the right prep school, owned a tuxedo (insistently called a "dinner jacket" by my parents), was well-spoken, and had a nice smile.

My mother went with me to choose my white dress, which had a fitted satin bodice with a portrait neckline and a huge tulle skirt. She insisted that I go to her own French hairdresser, Monsieur Jean, for a permanent wave, which I immediately hated. I wept all the way home from the salon. The professional photograph of me in my white dress shows me with firmly clenched teeth and an expression bordering on grim. Mum also bought me a girdle, which I hated even worse than the perm but which was much easier to ignore, as I could simply leave it off, which I did. I do not fault her now; Mum was, like any mother trying to do her best by introducing me to tokens of adulthood as she understood it. The permanent and the girdle were, to her, aspects of the painful initiatory rite.

The seating at the dinner was critical. As the nominal hostess, you placed boys you wanted to honor on either side, but this was tricky. The most favored boy was on your right and was expected to make a toast to you. This was an awesome responsibility. If someone who wasn't anticipating the honor were placed there, he could be scared away for good. On the other hand, you didn't want to encourage someone whose attentions you didn't welcome by so placing him. Seating someone on your left was much less fraught. I needed to discuss my own situation with my closest friends, thoroughly and many times. "Will you please stop tying up the phone?" my mother would eventually ask in exasperation.

In the three years since the Jim heartbreak, I had had several "beaux," as my mother liked to call them. Beaux will do as well as any other word here, as they were not "boyfriends" as the word is used in the 21st century, as there was no expectation of exclusivity, however temporary. These swains were just young men who asked me to play tennis, or go to the movies, or to a party, or sometimes to dinner. I had long correspondences with several of them while we were at boarding schools—writing letters was something I did in enforced study halls, and enjoyed. Getting mail was very important to us, as no telephoning was permissible or practical. With some of these boys, I did some low-key necking, but none of them made my heart beat faster—another expression of my mother's.

The previous summer in Northeast Harbor, and during the following winter and spring vacations of my senior year, I had gone out a few times with Bill Newlin, but he was by no means committed to me. I daydreamed about him constantly, but hesitated to put him on my right, even though he was my first choice. My friends told me to "keep him guessing." "Make him jealous," said Polly Gamwell, a boarding school friend who lived in New Jersey and who would be coming to my party. Burned by my first romance, I was inclined to take her advice. Polly came up with a strategy: we would explain the situation to her old friend George, whom I had met once or twice but who was unknown to Bill, and ask him to play a role. He was to be the mystery man, the guest of honor on my right, and I was to mention him frequently to Bill in the weeks before my party. Bill would be on my left.

This scheme worked very well in the weeks leading up to the party. Bill was wild with jealousy and curiosity about this unknown George who was to sit on my right, and his attentions to me intensified. The jig was up when George showed up the night of the party, as Bill perceived immediately that he was not nearly as charming, good-looking, tall, or intelligent as he himself. Triumphantly, he gave a much better toast than George's. This was my clear impression, although I no longer remember what either of them said. George, an affable young man, took all of this with good humor.

Since the unwritten rule was that every young man had to dance with the guest of honor, I had a whirl and felt pretty and admired. Even though I had not wanted a coming out party, I enjoyed mine thoroughly. It dawned on me only gradually that my parents had made sacrifices to give it. A week later, my mother said, "Your father has paid all the bills for the party and he feels much better." I felt a shock. My grandmother's house was free. Food and drink catered by Jimmy Duffy, a six-piece orchestra, flowers, a white ball dress, the services of Mrs. Thompson—these cost *money*? Belatedly, I thanked them both profusely, feeling guilty.

And what of Bill's *feelings* for me? The threat posed by George may have been temporary, but it did ratchet up the level of Bill's ardor. We became close during my freshman year at Radcliffe while he was a Harvard junior, and the June that he graduated, 1955, we were married. My parents thought we were too young, but were unable to protest very convincingly, having been married themselves at nineteen and twenty-one. They probably consoled themselves with the coming out parties having done their work: the marriage was endogamous, though they wouldn't have used the language of anthropology to say so.

THERE WERE TWO other ways of "coming out" that I haven't mentioned, both less expensive than giving a dance. One was to have a dinner before the Philadelphia Assembly in December and be presented at the ball as one of several debutantes. The Assembly has been given annually since 1748 and the wording on the invitation has remained as it was then, starting "It is proposed to hold a small assembly..." I believe the dress code is still the same: for women, full-length ball gowns, either with long sleeves and short white kid gloves, or short sleeves and elbow-length white kid gloves with buttons. Men wore white tie and tails. The ball has changed locations several times since its inception, but in my youth, it was in the Bellevue-Stratford Hotel downtown, in the Belle Epoque ballroom. A dozen ladies each year, the wives of prominent citizens from old Philadelphia families, were asked to be "patronesses" (this was an honor) and stood in a receiving line at the entrance to the ballroom, shaking the hands of everyone who came and addressing them by name. (There must have been a prompter near the head of the line supplying the names, which were then passed down from patroness to patroness.)

People invited to the Assembly, including my parents, were very proud of its exclusivity. There was a period in the 18th century when those "in trade" were not invited, and sometimes their descendants were excluded too, out of habit, though being in trade had long since lost its stigma by the mid-20th century, and at least half the included were in business of some kind. Out of town guests were welcome, but guests from in town could be invited only once. One could not apply for admission to the Assemblies; one had to wait until someone proposed you. I baited my mother about all this and asked her why she wanted to go to such a snobbish party. She said defensively, "It's the only time all year I get to go dancing all dressed up!" Even though this answer was probably not the whole truth, it makes more sense to me now than it did then. Since the 1950s, the guest list has grown much larger and the Assembly considerably democratized, I don't know to what extent.

My recollections of the Assembly that coming-out year are fuzzy. For reasons that remain obscure, perhaps having to do with a Newlin ancestor's having kept foxhounds (not Quakerly), or perhaps to do with Bill's father having been born in California, Bill's parents were not invited to the Assembly. This was a very sore point with his mother, who had been included before her marriage; a woman who married out of the Assembly , like a divorced woman, was summarily dropped. Gammy's brother and sister-in-law were Assembly-goers, which rankled.

The second time I went, the Christmas of my sophomore year at Radcliffe, I was already engaged to Bill and was allowed to take him as a guest and dancing partner. He was so handsome in his white tie and tails that I could not believe I was to marry such a stunning man. The ballroom scene looked like one in a Merchant Ivory film based on an Edith Wharton novel, and I really did want to dance all night: Meyer Davis was in peak form, conducting a full orchestra. His signature piece, played at full throttle, was "The Ride of the Valkyrie," to which we waltzed and waltzed until we were dizzy. I can't hear this music now without thinking of the Assembly, a curiously incongruous link to Wotan's warrior-maidens.

I have not mentioned the heart-pounding excitement of all these dances, or the pure joy of moving in time to music with a partner, or the sense that suddenly something wonderful might happen. When, as a freshman at Radcliffe, I read *War and Peace* for my Humanities 2 course, I was astonished by the description of Natasha Rostov at her first dance: scared, keyed up, dazzled, ready to fall in love. How did Tolstoy *know* how an adolescent girl would feel? I did not give him credit for imagination, the capacity that all novelists must have to succeed in creating character.

The other non-dance way of coming out was the Tea, often given by a grandmother, which was sometimes a tea-dance. While less glamorous than an evening party, the tea "counted" as a debut, and the society pages of the *Philadelphia Evening Bulletin* and *Philadelphia Inquirer* (there were *two* newspapers then) would have, as they did for the evening dances, a little story about the event, headlined something like "Julia Biddle Bows at Tea," featuring a picture of a pretty, smiling, young girl with neat hair. Not content with co-hosting the dance with my parents, Danny, who always wanted things done "properly," gave me a tea, primarily to meet her friends, and they all sent either flowers or evening bags as presents.

I couldn't imagine how I would ever use all those evening bags, and surreptitiously returned most for credit at Wanamaker's or Bonwit Teller. The ubiquitous Mrs. Thompson was on hand to keep a list of who had sent what, and I obediently wrote thank you notes to everyone. This was good practice for the wedding presents to be received two years later.

When our daughter Eliza graduated from Sidwell Friends in 1979, my mother was distressed that we had no plans for her to come out. No one in Eliza's class was coming out; it was not something girls at Quaker schools did. Mum took things into her own hands and planned a coming out tea for Eliza in Chestnut Hill, at Beechen Green. She invited friends of hers and Dad's and a collection of young people from Chestnut Hill and the Main Line, including the grandchildren of her friends. Mrs. Thompson had retired by then, but one of her heirs helped Mum out with a supplementary List of both boys and girls. Mum kept telephoning Eliza and asking her, "Are you sure you don't want any of your Washington friends invited?" Eliza would have died rather than let her Sidwell classmates know about the tea, so she kept politely declining. Poor Mum. It is the fate of grandmothers to want to give things that grandchildren don't want. It was a nice party, though, and there are pictures to prove it.

Bill and I gave a dance for the whole family that year, on June 16, in the ornate marble ballroom at Anderson House in Washington. After we had set the date, chosen because it was a Saturday in mid-June, son Bill realized that this date is "Bloomsday," the date on which Leopold Bloom lives through 24 hours in Dublin, in *Ulysses*. The lettering on the invitations was Irish green and invited the guests to a "Bloomsday Party."

Each of our children invited fifty of their friends and Bill and I invited a hundred. It was a smash. As I sat at a table with my brother Walter, he kept ribbing me, saying, "It sure *looks* like a coming-out party." But it wasn't, not really.

chapter ten

SPRINGSIDE

S pringside School, where I went from seventh through ninth grade, was not beside a spring. It was an unprepossessing fieldstone structure, formerly a private house, at the intersection of East Chestnut Hill Avenue and Bethlehem Pike. The walk to school was good for me, I was told, and I got plenty of exercise walking the mile there, mostly uphill, and the mile back, mercifully downhill. The houses of people I knew were landmarks along the way. Not long after starting up West Chestnut Hill Avenue came the Wetherills' house, then the Prices'. Next I passed a big estate now owned by a group of nuns, Carmelite sisters. (When it was sold to them, a rumor went around that it had been sold to a group of *Communist* sisters, which got my friends and me excited for a brief spell—Radicals in Chestnut Hill!—until the rumor was quashed.) Andy Oliver Young's house was on the right, after a dip down and a rise back up, and my friend and classmate Jennie Brown, whose family was English, lived on the left shortly after Andy Oliver's. I'd pass our doctor's office; inexplicably, Dr. McLannahan used to call me "Big Boy," which he thought a joke but which embarrassed me, especially when I began to develop breasts. Just before crossing Germantown Avenue, there was a walled garden behind a brick house which intrigued me. It made me think of *The Secret Garden*, and I longed to peep over the wall, which I was too short to do. When I did get a chance, years later, to look through an open gate at the garden, it was dusty and disappointing.

On Mondays, violin lesson days, I had to tote my instrument as well as my bookbag, and this I found intolerably burdensome, especially since I had the lesson at the Lingelbachs' house, which added an extra half mile or so on the way home. When I grumbled, my mother, completely unsympathetic would give me Yan's line, "You have a hard life." I did get rides on rainy days, though. Mostly.

Since most of the girls I had been to Miss Zara's with went on to Springside, I don't remember the transition as being difficult. I found it exciting to meet a whole new group of girls from Lower Springside and a few from other schools, including Joan Rosenbaum and Joan Mathieson, who became two of my closest friends. Joan R.

had transferred from Germantown Friends, where, she said, "if you don't have holes in your clothes at that school, you have to cut them." Joan Mathieson lived near Bethayres, a country village an hour away. Her friend and Bethayres neighbor Balene Cross, another new classmate, was already a great beauty, and aroused both admiration and envy; she had already been to the movies with a boy, tantamount to having a boyfriend.

We moved to different classrooms during the day, much more than we had at Miss Zara's, and school was therefore less claustrophobic. We had Mrs. Corson for Home Room in seventh grade and as our English teacher for both seventh and eighth. Only in her twenties, she was a born teacher, demanding but fair. She enjoyed the company of adolescent girls and had a sense of humor. She provided stability, continuity, acceptance, and fun. The books she chose struck chords with us: *The Yearling* and *Treasure Island* in the seventh grade, *A Tale of Two Cities* in eighth, *Romeo and Juliet* in the ninth. Even though I tended to read ahead and finish the book before the class had finished "discussing" it, and would therefore daydream in class and regularly have to be called back to earth, I adored her.

Miss Steinmetz, energetic, short, wiry-haired and brisk, taught us math, which she made tolerable. She also directed the chorus and was committed to introducing unfamiliar serious music—no more Stephen Foster songs. She "made us sing Mahler and shot us into Schutz," as Louise Purves later put it.

Mademoiselle Péchin taught us French. Although she looked like the old war horse of a teacher that she was—gray hair in a bun, glasses, standard-issue shapeless dun-colored dress, high black laced shoes—she was progressive in her approach to learning. We memorized all the verbs that take "être" instead of "avoir" to form the past tense by physicalizing them, Mlle Péchin leading the way: going up and down imaginary stairs (monter, descendre), in and out the real door (aller, revenir) and bravely falling down on the floor to die (morir.) We particularly appreciated *morir*. She served us well—we never forgot those verbs.

Mrs. Racy, who must have gone shopping with Mademoiselle Péchin, only she favored purple rather than dun, introduced us to first-year Latin gently, over a two-year period, starting in the eighth grade. Latin was catnip to me, as was Mrs. Racy's Alabama drawl. We could tell she loved her subject and loved us, and we returned the compliment.

Most interesting of all was the Physiology course given us in the seventh grade by Mrs. Parminter, a middle-aged mother of grown children. We studied the human body, and there was a four-week unit on menstruation and reproduction. We were of course endlessly curious about sex, and Mrs. Parminter's course cleared up several mysteries, one in particular. My mother had always been forthright with me; she often said this was because her own mother had not told her anything at all about sex, she'd had to find out everything from books and friends. However, I had not asked her a key question that had bothered me for quite a while: how on earth did a little limp thing like a penis, ever get into a vagina to do its work? I had seen my younger brothers undressed and, on the evidence of their equipment, could not for the life of me figure out the mechanics of this act said to occur between men and women and which was necessary for the creation of babies. Back in Cape May, Lois Upham and I, both with younger brothers and both baffled, had drawn pictures for each other of how intercourse might work, but we failed to come up with anything that looked credible. Mrs. Parminter, along with a little book that she distributed, explained it all matter-of-factly, with explicit diagrams. We could not imagine ourselves ever actually *doing* any of what was described—the very thought of an erect penis, let alone the illustration of one, had many of us either doubling over with hysterical laughter or making disgusted faces and saying "Ew!" but it was good to feel we understood some basic truths at last. It was not until the late sixties, when women everywhere began complaining about being left in ignorance throughout their teens, that I realized how ahead of their time both Springside and my mother had been.

Mrs. Parminter's course was timed to precede our first menstruation, assumed to be at twelve, but I had already started, at age eleven, shortly before entering seventh grade. Despite my mother's openness, I was shy about admitting this to my classmates. There were many whispered inquiries about who had "gotten it," and I was ahead of most people. Mum told me to be proud, but I wasn't.

Why was this? Is shame about our sexual development built in? Or did the societal hush about these matters at midcentury outbalance my mother's teachings? We could be excused from sports the first day of a period, occasionally the second, and although I was tempted by the possibility of missing hockey or lacrosse for a day, I chose to play, rather than admit to having my period.

Love was much on our pubescent minds; menstruating or pre-menstrual, we were emotionally right on schedule. We needed to fall in love. We didn't have much chance to socialize with boys and these feelings had to go somewhere. It was the fashion at Springside for seventh-graders to develop crushes on senior girls. I don't think we knew the word "lesbian" at the time—Mrs. Parminter's course did not deal with same-sex attraction. In any case, these crushes were not really lesbian in nature, more a yearning to be *like* the crushee, someone older, someone more glamorous, someone who went on dates, had a driver's license, and smoked at parties. Each of us picked a particular senior to admire, and told our friends who it was, so when that girl walked by, the friends would giggle and poke the supposedly infatuated one, who would blush. In my heart, I had no romantic interest in the senior I picked, or any other girl, but went along with the fad. My crush's first name was Jody, no doubt a perfectly nice girl, but the reason I chose her was that she wasn't already "taken." I don't think the seniors had any idea of all this and would have been astounded if they had, and probably a little embarrassed.

We may not have had the terminology, but we were aware of the atypical relationship between Miss Steinmetz—the aforementioned math and music teacher—and Miss Lowe, who lived together. Miss Lowe taught English to grades 10-12 and was universally respected. (I never had her as a teacher, since I went to boarding school in the tenth grade.) She was famous for being "hard" and taught only the strongest students, which the school allowed her to do because she was so valued. Then there was Miss Varre, the head sports coach, who was British and popular with the athletes but not with me. There was a time when, talking to a group of parents about why they should come to the games, she said, her face glowing, "You would so *love* to see your girls running up and down the field, getting all warm and sweaty." This made me uneasy for reasons I could not identify at the time. She clearly adored Jennie Brown, but we did not see anything strange in this, as Jennie was the hockey star of our class. Jennie's family moved back to England when their daughters had finished school and Jennie went on to become first a teacher at a girls' boarding school there and then its headmistress. She never married, and lived—still lives—with another woman. I have no reason to think that Miss Varre ever laid a hand on Jennie, but did she recognize a kinship?

One last teacher-memory. When we were in the ninth grade, we were at the top rung of middle school, soon to be knocked down from our perches when we went once more to the bottom of the upper-school ladder as tenth-graders. In the meantime, we were cocky about our status and entirely obnoxious. For Social Studies ("What did they do with History and Geography?" my father asked grumpily) we had a young teacher fresh out of Wellesley, with no previous teaching experience. I'll call her Miss Dempsey. Unlike beloved Mrs. Corson, she was not a natural. We smelled her insecurity and tormented her heartlessly, interrupting her to ask silly questions, shamelessly passing notes and whispering to each other in class. She tried to control us by stopping class and glaring, but it did no good. We only smirked and nudged each other. The only thing I remember learning from her is how to do an oral report, using notes on 3x5 cards. They were to be on some aspect of British history or geography. We were graded on presentation as well as content, and told to stand still and straight, without fidgeting, make eye contact, sound enthusiastic, and start off with a punchy lead. I can still see Martha Kolb, a stocky, cheerful, pink-faced girl, looking out at her classmates and saying with great energy, "To miss East Anglia is to miss the rolling chalk fields of England!" We couldn't help laughing aloud. Miss Dempsey married in the middle of the year and became Mrs. Weston, which made her seem older. She stuck it out, and some years after I'd left the school, I heard she had become a popular and respected teacher. It made me feel bad about the way we had hazed her, but perhaps we actually helped her by toughening her up.

WE HAD TO wear uniforms, which at first I did not mind: navy skirts, white shirts and either yellow or navy sweaters. (Blue and Gold were the school colors.) The older girls, tenth grade and above, wore gray blazers. There were very few days when we seventh graders actually wore these skirts, however, as on sports days we wore medium blue pleated tunics, and we had sports most days. The tunics were not to be more than two inches above the knee and were worn with black stockings held up by garter belts, concealed by black bloomers which made sure no white flesh or garters showed when we ran. Brown tie shoes and white ankle socks, over the black stockings, completed the outfit, one I was very ready to abandon at the end of ninth grade.

Sports were required, and the athletes were the unquestioned aristocrats. Field hockey, Springside's fall sport, was torture for me, especially the long afternoons devoted to what was called "Squad", which meant *extra* after-school hockey practice. There were only two athletic fields at the school so, for Squad, we were bused to some other school's field, usually several miles distant. Including time spent on the bus both ways, the Squad afternoons could last until five-thirty. I consoled myself for the loss of time I would have rather spent reading with the knowledge that I was sharing something with the aristocrats and would be able to chime in on hockey conversations over lunch. Squad was voluntary, but I signed up for it because for taking it, you got extra points towards your chevron, a blue and yellow patch to sew on a sweater, awarded at the end of the year on Prize Day.

The point system was complicated. You accumulated points throughout the year, and you could lose points for cheating or tardiness, or some other transgression like rudeness. Some activities were worth more than others. There were points for all extra sports practices, but none given for things I did best: English, Latin, and French. When I asked Mrs. Corson why, she said, "Because some girls, no matter how hard they work, can not do well in academic subjects." "But Mrs. Corson," I said, " no matter how many hours I spend at Squad, I'm not going to be a hockey star. "You can get points for Citizenship," Mrs. Corson suggested doubtfully, knowing full well that I had no natural talent for that, either, or for School Spirit, which was worth a lot of points, though how it was measured I wasn't sure.

I did a little better in basketball in the winter, and, surprisingly, at lacrosse in the spring. But my hockey never improved much. There were five hockey teams. Jennie Brown was the youngest member of the First Team, and stayed on it right through senior year. I was on the Fifth Team in seventh grade, and on the Fourth in eighth and ninth. We played other girls' schools in the Philadelphia area: Agnes Irwin, Shipley, Baldwin, and girls' teams from coeducational schools like Germantown Friends. The best of the Fourth Team athletes played Center or one of the Inners; I played Left Wing for a couple of years, trying desperately to keep the ball from going out and trying to pass it to one of our heroic Inners. Then in ninth grade, I tried Goalie, a position in which I foolishly imagined

I would be able to stand still and think. This was even worse, as I earned the team's opprobrium when I failed to block a goal, which was often. Ironically, Farmington, the school I went to post-Springside, was far less a "jock" school, and there I was considered a pretty good player. But it was a happy day when I finally went to college and could fulfill the athletic requirements with tennis, which I played competently, archery, and bowling. For these last two, no change of clothes was required, a bonus.

I sometimes had trouble getting to school on time, mostly because I didn't leave early enough. Each tardiness earned you some sort of black mark, and when you'd accumulated a dozen or so, you had to report to the principal for sentencing, usually to a few hours of Saturday School. I remember only one such punishment. We reported for duty and sat down in the study hall at desks. Then some luckless teacher assigned to oversee the transgressors presented us with copies of Shelley's "Ozymandias" and instructed us to write a paper about it. I'd never read the poem and immediately found it fascinating. I enjoyed writing about it, and still had more to say when I'd served my time. It was a classic case of throwing Bre'r Rabbit into the briar patch.

A much more serious transgression was the one and only time I ever plagiarized. We were to write a short story for English, and, under the spell of a story I had read recently by Elizabeth Goudge, I helped myself to her plot. I don't remember the title or indeed anything about it except that there was a handsome and dashing character in a cape and boots, possibly a feathered hat as well, who turned out to be a personification of Death. This seemed like such a great idea that I wanted it to be my own. I was a good writer and could easily have written something original, but I wanted desperately to have written *this* story.

I wrote it in my own words and handed it in to my English teacher, Mrs. Stevens. She gave me an A, and told me to submit it to the literary magazine, which, unwisely, I did. I was caught: someone on the literary magazine staff recognized the Goudge story, and asked me if I had read it. I confessed right away that I had, and felt humiliated beyond endurance. "My" story was of course not published. I have no recollection of other consequences, but I suppose I had to go back to my English teacher and tell her what I had done. My "A" was probably replaced with a zero, and I probably had to write a new story, but I don't remember anything dire happening to me -—no academic probation, not even Saturday School. I don't think anyone told my parents; I certainly didn't. What lingered was the intense feelings of embarrassment and shame which kept me from ever doing anything like that again.

MY BEST FRIENDS were Joan Rosenbaum, Anne Miller, and Joan Mathieson. In seventh grade, we called ourselves the "Fearless Four" and went out together trick-or-treating on Halloween. We dressed as the "Three Musketeers and d'Artagnan," who was a kind of musketeer-in-training; we knew this because we had read an abridgment of the novel in French class as well the Classic Comic. Several of the people we collected candy expressed amusement at having *four* musketeers at their door. This surprised us; we thought everyone knew about d'Artagnan.

When Louise Purves came back from Mexico, in the eighth grade, we became the "Fearless Five." We eventually dropped the name, feeling it was no longer cool, but remained close friends, even though we lived in different neighborhoods. Only Anne and I lived in Chestnut Hill proper, and Anne's house, on Benezet Street (referred to often as "Bassinet Street" because of the preponderance of families with babies living there) was too far from mine for a comfortable walk. Louise Purves and Joan Rosenbaum both lived in different parts of Germantown, an easy trolley ride from Chestnut Hill. Joan Matheison lived in the country, an hour's drive away, so when we got together on weekends, either she was driven to one of our houses and slept over or we were driven to hers. Her mother, Mrs. Lippincott, was always hospitable; Joan had two sisters, old enough to have left home, and her mother did not want her youngest to feel isolated.

In one place or another, at least three of us would get together on Saturdays. We were allowed the run of Chestnut Hill and often went to the matinee at the Hill movie theater, now defunct. Movies having been so strictly rationed in my life so far, the freedom of seeing them with a group of friends and without parents was exhilarating. My mother always knew exactly what was playing and knew also that the Hill Saturday matinees were free of "adult content." (Movies in general were a lot tamer then.) I remember "Gunga Din" making a strong impression on me; I was amazed to see that a whole movie could be made out of Kipling's poem.

Often we went to Germantown, where we were supposed to stay within certain boundaries near Joan Rosenbaum's or Louise's house. The Rosenbaums lived in large, curlicued yellow Victorian house in a neighborhood that had been the height of fashion in the 1880s but which was now slipping; the Rosenbaums could have afforded to move but loved the house and hung on where they were. Their family seemed much more interesting than mine or than the families of the others. Joan's mother, Edna Phillips, a harpist, was the first woman to be admitted to the Philadelphia Orchestra and Joan enjoyed a lot of reflected glory. She showed me a clipping from her mother's scrapbook with a picture of herself as a baby and a headline, "Joan Rosenbaum to Make Concert Tour in Basket." Joan had interesting half-sisters in their twenties who lived in England, as well as a younger brother, David. Mr. Rosenbaum was a cultivated man, a patron of the arts who loved all forms of what he called "serious" music. When Joan was in the eighth or ninth grade, he and Mrs. Rosenbaum (she used the name Edna Phillips only professionally) gave her a coeducational birthday party at which the entertainment was a performance by two opera singers of Gian Carlo Menotti's "The Telephone," short and funny but nevertheless, it was the proverbial pearls before swine; the male guests had a hard time sitting still.

On most evenings, after supper and homework, I talked on the phone to at least two of these friends, sometimes to all four. We had to check up on what everyone else had been doing since they got home from school, who else they had talked to on the phone and what they said, whether they'd had a problem with the math. We had to discuss what someone we didn't like had said at lunch that day, whether they had seen a particular boy somewhere on the way home, and, during the periods immediately following a Friday Evening Dancing Class, who now "liked" whom. These calls were extremely important to us; being called was a sign of acceptance. My parents tried to be patient and understanding of junior high school needs, but they had only one telephone line—no one without a home office had more—and occasionally they were exasperated, and told me to just for heaven's sake, hang up, *now*.

Because the period when my friends turned into enemies was so painful, I have a hard time remembering the details. I am not sure even whether it happened during the spring of eighth grade or of ninth. Probably the latter, as we had begun having occasional mixed parties at which boys and girls slow-danced to records, in the dark, until some parent came and turned the lights on. A boy named Alex had been paired with another member of in our Springside class, a girl I'll call Carol. She was not one of our little clique but friendly with it. Alex may not even have realized he was thought of as Carol's boyfriend. He danced with me a lot during one of these parties, ignoring Carol, and decided he liked me instead, or so he told one of his friends, who told his sister, who told someone in our class.

This "liking" manifested itself in a few phone calls from Alex, an invitation to a movie (chaperoned by his parents,) and a box of writing paper on my birthday. But, in the eyes of my friends, I had "stolen" Carol's boyfriend, an unpardonable sin, and for committing it, I was ostracized by my friends for several dreadful weeks. (There were probably other reasons for my being suddenly shunned, but I have never known what they were.) No one would call me, and if I called them, they would not talk to me. "We've made a pact," one of them explained. My mother knew something was wrong. "Is there anything you want to talk about?" she would ask anxiously, and I lied that everything was fine. It was too mortifying to have lost my friends.

I got sick. I developed a bad eye infection and ran a fever that kept me at home and in bed. I had a big patch over the infected eye, and was not supposed to read with the other, for fear of eyestrain. (I don't think people worry so much any more about eyestrain.) I listened to daytime radio soap operas and was old enough to be embarrassed about this; I would turn the volume down low when somebody came in my room. Each of them had a sudsy sponsor (Ivory Flakes, which were oh-so gentle; Lava, to deal with grit and grime; Fels-Naptha, to wash with after poison ivy; Duz, which "does everything") and each show was introduced with a tag, often a question the drama would answer. For "Helen Trent" it was "Can a woman over thirty still find happiness in love?" and for "Our Gal Sunday," "Can a little girl from a silver mining town in Colorado find happiness as the wife of one of England's richest and most famous Lords?" Despite my better judgment, the stories sucked me in, and distracted me from my misery.

I could not face going back to school and managed to prolong this illness for a couple of weeks. The eye infection itself cleared up in a week or so, but I continued to stay sick. In the morning, my mother would come in and take my temperature, and I can remember trying to *will* a low fever and succeeding. Or maybe it was there without my willing it. I am pretty sure, though, that it was my unhappiness kept me physically sick, and knew this at the time. I could not figure out what to do. I couldn't call Alex and tell him he wasn't my boyfriend any more, since he never knew that he was.

Finally, there was a thaw. Joan Mathieson was the first to break the pact of silence with the others. She called me on the phone, and kindly caught me up with what was going on at school. She must have interceded on my behalf with Anne, Louise, and the other Joan, as they consented to talk to me when I called them. My temperature returned to 98.6. I rose from my bed and returned to school. Carol had a new boyfriend, and my supposed theft of Alex was no longer interesting. Life returned to normal, as normal as it gets in junior high school, but I lived it with a new wariness. When I went off to boarding school in the tenth grade, I went reluctantly, but with a half-acknowledged feeling of gratitude at the chance to make a fresh start.

FARMINGTON

I n the fall of 1950, at the start of my 10th grade year, I was sent to Miss Porter's School, a boarding school for about 260 girls. It was known then as "Farmington," the name of the village in which the school was located, nine miles west of Hartford, Connecticut. It did not look institutional, except for the gym, which doubled as a meeting hall and a theater—there was a raised stage at one end. There was no clearly defined campus. The dormitories, lining both sides of Main Street, were large frame New England houses of the late 19th and early 20th centuries, all different in style and color. Even the brick administration building and the library were converted houses. The village is still picturesque, its streets shaded by old oaks and maples, its lawns lush.

Farmington inspired great affection in many of its graduates, although, sadly, never in me. Main Street was at that period a heavily traveled major route, and we were under orders to cross only between the two yellow lines guarded by Miller, the school's very own policeman. I came to think of this as symbolic: the price of our safety from on-rushing traffic was staying within those clearly defined lines.

My mother had been to Farmington, graduating in 1933, and thrived there. For her, it offered a liberation from the routines and demands of her loving and deeply conservative family. She had been one of the school leaders, head of the student government, which was called "Little Meeting" because of its origins as a "little meeting" in the room of a student who thought students should have some say in the running of the school. (Thanks to Little Meeting, students had more say than they had earlier, but even twenty years later, they still did not have much.) Mum stayed on for a post-graduate year which she liked to maintain was the equivalent of a year of college, which it was not—except for the Art History course, taught by the redoubtable Miss McLennan, who was, fortunately, still around to teach me. By the time of her "postgrad" year, Mum's class was down to 30; the Depression forced many parents to pull their daughters out of private school. My mother remained loyal to Farmington throughout her life and went to reunions yearly until she was the only attendee in her class. I'm sure it was a lasting sorrow to her that I never felt the same way she did about the school.

There had never been any question in my parents' mind that I would go to Farmington. During my ninth-grade year at Springside, my mother took me up to the school so that I could look it over and vice versa, but since half of the students were the daughters of alumnae, and since my grades at Springside were good, there was no suspense about my being admitted. During this inspection tour, I visited an English class taught by Miss Comans, who later became a favorite of mine; she was teaching Shelley's "The Indian Serenade" and the music of the opening lines immediately bewitched me.

I arise from dreams of thee
In the first sweet sleep of night,
When the winds are breathing low,
And the stars are shining bright.

Hearing those lines for the first time, listening to a discussion of it—the moment has stayed with me.

MY FATHER HAD his own reasons for sending me to Farmington: he did not want me to date, and said so. I would have rather stayed at home and continued at day school, but, given some of my troubles with friends at Springside, I thought getting a fresh start wasn't a bad idea. A couple of good friends, Joanie Mathieson and Robin Boyer, were going to Farmington too, and there would be more Shelley with Miss Comans. So I went off without much protestation.

The school, established in 1847, had been until the 1940s, a finishing school for young ladies who were not expected to go on to further education. They acquired there an acquaintance with literature, history, art history, French, Latin, and music, all of which theoretically prepared them to make conversation with the boys they would meet when they "came out"—which in those days, and in my day too, meant making your début. By the time I got there, Farmington was a college preparatory school with a curriculum that included mathematics (only through Algebra II, no calculus) and sciences (ecology, biology, and chemistry at basic levels). Classes were smaller than they had been at Springside, and it was harder to get away with daydreaming and note-passing. By 1950, most graduates did go to college, though many went to two-year "junior colleges," most of which have since become four-year colleges or disappeared altogether. We were not being prepared for careers, however; the general expectation was that we would become model wives, mothers, and volunteer community leaders. Careers were for women who did not marry.

My mother drove me up to school that first September. I arrived as a sophomore, as did nearly all the girls. Our class numbered about eighty, including twenty who had been there for ninth grade, so although the school was roughly the same size overall as Springside, which went from kindergarten through twelfth grades, I had nearly three times as many classmates. It was stimulating to have so many new friends from New York, Chicago, Detroit,

Minneapolis, Milwaukee, San Francisco, even Honolulu. One of our school songs referred to Farmington as "Where the girls from all the world/With each other meet," which became hard for me to sing with a straight face. There was a degree of geographic diversity, but ethnically, everyone was Caucasian and Protestant, except for two dozen Catholics. (My last year, one of the incoming sophomores was rumored to be Jewish. She was Nathan Milstein's daughter, but she attended the Congregational church—church of some kind was required.) Not much diversity socio-economically either—there were a few doctors and teachers among the fathers, but most were businessmen, bankers, or lawyers. Most of the mothers occupied themselves as wives, mothers, and volunteers for non-profit organizations, though there were a few who painted or who had small interior-decorating businesses. There were some scholarship students, usually the daughters of alumnae who had fallen on hard times. It took me three years to absorb all this, and even then, I was past college when I realized how many of my classmates' names were, as Fitzgerald described those of girls at one of Gatsby's parties, those of the "great American capitalists." The names Rockefeller and DuPont were familiar, but McCormick, Weyerhauser, Gould, and so forth did not signify farm machinery, lumber, or railroads until much later.

While there was no uniform, there was a dress code: skirt, blouse with collar, sweater—sleeves could not be rolled up—tie shoes, brown or black, preferably "abercrombies" with the fringed flaps over the laces. Even in such a narrow slice of American society, there was a significant income range, and, in the interests of democratic appearances, the school legislated against competitive dressing. We were to bring no more than four skirts and six sweaters, although some girls inevitably brought contraband. (Fufa Triplett, brought thirty-two cashmere sweaters with her from Little Rock, Arkansas in anticipation of a long New England winter. She hid all but six under her bed.) We were to bring one outfit suitable for church on Sundays, including a hat, and two "dressier" dresses, to wear with stockings and high heels, to Saturday night entertainment in the gym. These could not be low-cut, either in the front or the back, and if Mrs. Johnson, the headmaster's wife, determined that either V was cut too deep, she would oblige the dress's owner to patch in modesty triangles. No make up, not even lipstick, was permitted, nor were earrings. A friend with pierced ears tried to keep the holes open by wearing safety pins, but these were quickly disallowed. I am not exactly sure what the rationale for categorically denying us makeup and earrings was, other than simply slowing down our growing- up, but when I look around at little girls of ten and eleven imitating teenage pop stars, I understand the impulse behind the prohibitions. The rules made putting on lipstick during vacations thrilling. What I later called "the utility of foolish rules" was operative: since teenagers need desperately to rebel, it is in a school's interest to have an array of rules that it will do young people no harm to break. If there are no foolish rules to break, they may resort to trying out drugs, sex, or truancy, which could cause them lasting damage.

Many of the rules were common to all such institutions of that era: no smoking, no drinking—other drugs had not yet even been thought of. No leaving the school "bounds" without permission, except to walk to a sweet shop called the Gundy or to the belt shop in the village, where we could buy decorated leather belts to set off our tiny waists. Other rules seemed designed only to seal us off from the wider world: no radios in our rooms, record-players (Victrolas) for seniors only, played only at designated times.

Newspapers were available in the library, but few read them except in fulfilling a specific homework assignment. Television was not available anywhere, but as this was only just beginning to be a household item, we didn't miss it. No telephone calls, even to parents, except in extreme emergencies. Parents could call us, but this was discouraged, as you had to be summoned to Brick, the administration building, to receive it at a hall phone.

Occasional telegrams were permitted. Joanie and her mother worked out a code: if Joan sent a telegram saying "I have the hiccups," her mother was to call her. Once she sent a telegram saying "I have a terrible case of the hiccups." Her mother had temporarily forgotten all about the code, and called the school in a panic, wanting to know if Joan had been hospitalized. Midway through a conversation with the receptionist, she remembered, and said, "Oh never mind, it's all right, I just want to talk to my daughter."

There was obligatory study hall every evening after dinner, except Saturdays and Sundays, and no letter writing during it. (I got very good at writing letters on lined paper that made them look like compositions, adding salutation and closing later, in private.) Once homework was finished, you had to stay in study hall but could read for pleasure, which is why I was able to read so many books during those three years. *Crime and Punishment, Tess of the d'Urbervilles, Wuthering Heights,* and much popular fiction whose titles have washed out of my head. Seniors could study in their rooms, which was bliss. We were not supposed to visit back and forth during the study hall hours, though of course we did. A lot of semi-legal intense bridge-playing went on, so much that I never played again after I left the school.

Both administration and teachers regarded parents as dangerous distractions who could visit only on certain weekends. Since we had Saturday morning classes, these visits were necessarily short. The highlight of a parental visit was being taken out to Sunday lunch at the Corner House, the inn where most parents stayed. Boys were even more dangerous distractions and "callers," no more than one per term, were allowed to visit between 2 and 4 pm on "open" Saturday afternoons. With your caller, you could walk around the campus but could not sit down anywhere. Canoodling may not have been explicitly banned, but the context made it hard. Promptly at 4 pm, you had to check in to the Johnsons' house for tea with any other girls with callers—otherwise, scouts went out to retrieve you—and at precisely 4:45, the caller was sent firmly on his way. Decamping before tea was frowned on and the caller placed on a blacklist, never to return. Few young men of my acquaintance could brave this ordeal. The only time I remember having a caller was when Bill made it down from Harvard, with a friend, the spring term of my senior year, and we managed some sit-down canoodling behind a gravestone in the cemetery.

Back to the beginning: my first year, I was in a house called Ward, with 30 or so other sophomores. I shared a room with a wide-eyed girl even more innocent than most of us whom I will call Mary Ann; we got along tolerably well but never became close. She lacked the rebellious spirit that attracted me to the girls who became my real friends.

We had an anxious wall-eyed housemother, Miss Seymour, to watch over us. She was, in retrospect, pitiful— over sixty, drab, alone in the world, and obliged to take an unskilled position that offered her room and board. (The housemothers were not teachers; to most of the teachers we were more respectful.) Being young and pitiless, we made fun of poor Miss Seymour behind her back and were none too polite to her face.

We fell into the routine. Tuesday through Saturday, sit-down breakfast at assigned tables, each presided over by a teacher, prayers in the living room, a hymn, and often a homily given by the headmaster, Mr. Johnson. Those sitting in the front row were not to cross their legs. Farmington was a consciously Christian school, though not affiliated with a particular denomination. Academic classes followed until the sit-down lunch at an assigned table, interrupted by a 20-minute morning break with a snack of milk and crackers to keep us going. In the afternoon, non-academic classes like studio art or play rehearsals, sports (required of all), free time before dinner, seated dinner, study hall, lights out by 9 pm. Quiet talking in the dark with one's roommate until 10.

Sundays and Monday until dinner were less routinized. Breakfast was buffet and sit-where-you-like, and the dress code was relaxed. We could even wear blue jeans. Saturday nights we dressed up and, if there was no lecture or performance planned for us, we entertained each other by singing songs from Broadway musicals or old music-hall numbers, in duets or quartets. An *a capella* group called the Perhilettes used to do "Mood Indigo" to wild applause. Cinny Earling, a born clown from Milwaukee, and I used to make everyone laugh with "How Could You Believe Me When I Said I Loved You, When you Know I've Been a Liar All My Life." There were some solos too; we used to melt at Bitsy Large's clear soprano rendition of "Come to me, Bend to me" from "Brigadoon" which spoke to all our romantic dreams of the passionate undying love which would some day be ours.

I was not made miserable by Farmington, but I had enjoyed a freedom in Chestnut Hill which made me feel claustrophobic at boarding school. As sophomores, "new girls," we were allowed only one "short weekend" away from the school. Short weekends went from Saturday after classes to Monday afternoon at 5 pm (The free Monday was fine if you were going home or to someone's house, but if you were visiting a boys' school or college, you had to figure out what on earth to do with Monday. Your date certainly didn't want you around after Sunday afternoon.) Juniors were granted one short weekend during the year and one "long weekend," which started Friday afternoon after classes and went until Monday afternoon. Seniors got two long weekends away and one short, as well as a Saturday afternoon shopping in West Hartford. No more than one weekend could be taken in each of the three terms, and furthermore, many weekends were "closed," like the ones before and after vacations and before the weeks when major tests were given. One oddity: there were no exams, only papers and period-long tests at intervals. The rationale was that exams were a poor measure of what you had learned, which might have been true, but it left us ill-prepared for the intensity, length, and terror of exams in college.

These weekends away were crucially important to us. They were the only times we saw boys—legally, anyway, except for the largely non-existent callers. The answer to "Where are you going for your weekend?" could confer status or the reverse. Most prestigious was to be going as someone's date to a dance weekend at one of the boys' prep schools or, better yet, to a college football weekend. Girls would return from these weekends with trophies—long, knitted scarves striped with the colors of the relevant school or college. Girls who owned multiple scarves—collected rather like scalps—became legends of popularity.

In our collective opinion, "Going home" for your week-end, or to someone else's home, was a poor substitute, an admission of defeat and unpopularity. "Popularity" was a key word during those years. When you were going to a dance weekend, you could subsist, emotionally, on antic-ipation for weeks ahead and on recollection for months afterward. (In my case, the recollection of my first dance weekend, at Brooks School, with Joe Wear, was acutely painful, as it was during it that he dumped me, after which I fell into a prolonged depression.)

Colleges and boys' boarding schools were ranked: you got many more status points for being invited to St. Paul's or Exeter than to Westminster or Brooks, for instance, and more for going to Princeton, Yale, or Harvard than to Williams or Amherst. In the fall, foot-ball games were the focal points. (In fact, I did not like watching football games at all, but did not realize it was possible to admit this out loud until I was at college and found my feelings shared by numerous others. Liking football was not the point.) The *particular* game you were invited to was significant. The fall of my senior year, Bill invited me to the Harvard-Davidson game, which did not have the prestige of the Harvard-Yale game. I won-dered whom he had invited to the big one. That year, the Harvard-Yale game was at Yale, an hour's bus ride away, and the school emptied out. I'd used up my fall weekend on the Davidson game. One of the teachers, probably Mrs. Karstens, arranged for us left-behinds to go Hart-ford and see "American in Paris," new that year. We were transported. *This is the way real life is supposed to be*, I thought, as I watched Leslie Caron and Gene Kelley dancing around the city and falling in love.

The school motto translated from the Latin was "We came as girls, we left as women." An exaggeration, since at seventeen or eighteen, we were hardly real adults. Cooped up as we were, our teachers had perhaps more influence over our ideas of what might mean to be a woman in 1953 than those at day schools. We were not sure we wanted to be like our mothers, and we certainly did not want to become *like* our female teachers, even the good ones who exerted a positive influence on us.

There were some far too old for us to imagine ever wanting to be like them. Three of these, Mlle. Nédelec (French), Miss Shapleigh (biology), and the aforementioned art historian Miss McClennan, had taught my mother. Mlle. Nédelec was famous for her susceptibility to derailment. ("Get her to tell you about the state funeral of Maréchal Foch," my mother had said, and I did; Mlle. N. described it to us for a whole forty- minute period while we happily egged her on with questions about horses and uniforms.)

Young, divorced Miss Karstens, our music teacher and spy in faculty meetings, described meetings in which each girl's name was brought up and her teachers assigned her a grade; Mlle. Nédélec, in the accent she never lost, would say of all her students, "She is such a nice girl. I will give her a B."

For Miss Shapleigh, biology consisted of endless lists to memorize, and since memorizing was easy for me and for my lab partner Sheila Hollern; we got good grades without working hard but were bored to distraction. Dissecting a frog provided some hands-on work which Sheila and I enjoyed, and we were scornful of those who made noises of disgust during the process. Miss Shapleigh's prize possession was a male fetus named Homer, pickled in formaldehyde, in a bottle kept on a top shelf in her back room; her voice became tender when she mentioned him, holding out a viewing as a potential reward for a good test grade. When I told a college friend about this later on, she asked, "Where did she get it?" I had no idea, and still don't. Better not to ask.

Miss McClennan was an unusually demanding teacher who knew her stuff and insisted that we know it too. She insisted we look at art objectively, rather than personally. Polly Gamwell was prone to saying, "Well, I'm sure it's good, but I wouldn't want it in my living room," and Miss McClennan would sigh deeply and say in her deep, intimidating voice, folding her arms across her chest and rocking back and forth and looking sternly over her glasses, "Polly, the criterion of art is NOT *your living room.*" The tone in which she said this suggested that although she had never seen the Gamwell living room, she had all too good an idea of what kind of art graced its walls, chosen for the way it picked up the colors in the chintz slipcovers. We knew Miss McClennan drank, as she often breathed whiskey into our faces as she bent over us to check our compositions, and undoubtedly she had other problems she was hiding from in a girls' boarding school. We were grateful to her for her high standards, and for the love of Renaissance art with which she imbued us, and grateful to the school for not firing her, but how could we wish to *be* her?

Miss Smedley, who taught us Modern European History, had also taught my mother. She had salt-and-pepper hair, and must have been in her late forties—Mum said that when she was there, Miss Smedley was brand new. She was wiry, energetic, knowledgeable, and creative. Her classes were fun and substantive both. But, like almost all the women teachers, she was not married, and married was something all of us wanted to be, *expected* to be, dreaded not being. Dark-eyed, dark-haired Miss Salzmann, who taught French 3 my first year, was an exception. It was her first teaching job, but she was a natural. She was bilingual—her father was from Alsace-Lorraine, though she had grown up in the U.S. Like Miss Smedley, she was enthusiastic and knew what would interest girls our age. I remember reading *Cyrano de Bergerac*, Daudet's *Lettres de Mon Moulin*, and a short story by Prosper Merimée called "Tamango" about an African chief who ends up in France playing the bass drum in a marching band. Miss Salzmann, alone among our teachers, had a sense of style. Her budget and her wardrobe were limited, but we observed how cleverly she put together the pieces of it in different ways—*French* ways—for a variety of Looks, and the chic way she tied her large collection of scarves which rivaled that of Mlle. Lambert at Miss Zara's. We could look at attractive Miss Salzmann and see a role model.

She shepherded groups of girls to tour France in the summers, and on one of these she met a Frenchman whom she happily married; she returned to Farmington for a year to fulfill her contract, but after that, she and her husband went to live in France. I hope she continued to teach there.

One of the teachers who came in by the day, a Mrs. Neilson, was married, but she was uninspiring and deep into middle age. Because of her fondness for deep blue and purple clothes, we referred to her as "the bruise" behind her back. One other teacher besides Mrs. Karstens had been married and divorced—Mrs. Wallace, an English teacher whose best friend was Miss Comans. They did not share the same apartment, but they clearly had a close relationship which led us to speculate in private about whether or not it was sexual. We did not use the word "lesbian" when talking about them.

There were a few men on the faculty, too, all of them married; I don't think the school administration would have dared to let a bachelor loose in that place. They liked us, and some were effective, but they had ideas about how women should look and behave which bothered me. Mr. French, who also taught French though never to me, used to say he hated women to wear flat shoes because their legs looked so much prettier when they wore high heels. Mr. Spear, an English teacher who loved Shakespeare and liked to read aloud all the best roles himself—it never occurred to him that a girl could read the part of Hamlet—was famous among us for unfailingly directing his gaze towards our breasts, even when calling on us in class. Never guilty of out-and-out sexual harassment (a term not yet in general use), he left no doubt about what our most interesting anatomical features were. We decided Mr. Spear was "oversexed." Our revenge was to joke a lot about him behind his back and about how his poor wife must be worn out from his attentions. The school doctor—a Dr. Bunnell—was more threatening, as we saw him alone and often he let his hands wander inappropriately during a physical exam. We tried to dispel our nervousness by calling him "old feely fingers," but would never have dared report him to anyone in power.

The head of the school was a man, Ward Johnson, who could be terrifying during one of his angry outbursts. I was the victim of one of these near the end of my first year. I no longer remember what brought it on, but his principal accusation was that I "was too big for my boots." He reduced me to tears and apologies (apologies for what? I wonder now), and then, just as inexplicably as he had exploded, he decided he was my supporter. I became one of his favorites, better for me than the opposite, but it's hardly a good policy for a headmaster to have obvious pets. He steered me to Radcliffe, along with Joanie Mathieson, Sheila Hollern, and four other friends, and for that I thank him, as on my own, I might not have thought of going there. He cited its proximity to MIT as a strong point in its favor. "Engineers," he said, "eat well." The implication was that I would be in good husband-hunting territory. I remember his saying admiringly of Joanie, "She thinks like a man." Thinking like a man was evidently the best way to think.

We were being educated to "think like women," not by our teachers, the best of whom tried hard to encourage aspirations beyond home, family, and parties, but by the zeitgeist of the 1950s. We were being educated to be wives, yes, and specifically to be ladies. Ladies wore hats and gloves in cities and when traveling; when we ladies-in-training went home for vacation, we were supposed to wear hats and gloves throughout the train journey, though we shed them in a hurry as soon as the train left the station, as we did on the journey back. We put them back on again just in time to meet the chaperone and the bus in West Hartford.

Farmington had the reputation of providing subliminal instruction in "dressing well." Prime examples of this art were Lee Bouvier Radziwell and her more famous sister, Jaqueline Bouvier Kennedy, recent graduates of the school whose photographs regularly appeared in *Vogue* and *Town and Country*. "Good taste" was the objective, not high fashion or expense. (High fashion was associated with "Café Society," the definition of which was unclear; it seemed to be a mixture of entertainers and social climbers in New York City, people who went to night clubs, wore a lot of make-up, and had pierced ears.) Cashmere sweater sets worn with pearls were safe, and polo coats, and well-cut dresses in muted pastels. Nothing too slinky. If you used a handbag, it should match your shoes. Girls who already knew "how to dress" were honored by being designated much-admired Ushers in the Gym, showing visitors to their seats at concerts, plays, and ceremonial events.

Joanie Mathieson, tall and willowy, who looked wonderful in anything she put on, was an Usher, even though she "thought like a man." She wore this honor gracefully.

In fairness, I should mention some of the highlights of my Farmington years. Writing for the *Salamagundi* literary paper (it was not a full-fledged magazine) was fun, as was working on the script for a musical version of *Toad of Toad Hall*, adapted from *The Wind in the Willows*. Another year, I worked on a musical version of James Thurber's *The Thirteen Clocks*. Both of these were for productions of the Mandolin Club, in which there were no mandolins; it was an instrumental club to which I had been assigned because I played the violin, the only girl in the school who did. Mrs. Karstens was our advisor, who made these productions possible.

The school is much more diverse than when I was there. It has remained committed to women's education, and although it lost applicants to the formerly all-male prep schools which went co-ed in the early 1970s, it has gained many from Asian and Middle Eastern families whose cultures favored single-sex education. There are more day students, and more opportunities to engage with a wider world. The dress code is more relaxed. There is a huge new gym and a state-of-the art theater, and the school's look is more institutional. The girls call it "Porter's" now, which my mother would detest.

Since we were confined to the school premises for weeks at a time, there was plenty of time to talk, talk, talk, in twos and threes and fours, on long walks, between classes, and after lights. (The presence of a teacher made us self-censor our talk at meals.) We talked a lot about boys, as we had at Springside: which boys had said what to which girls at holiday parties; who might have kissed whom, or more; who was going to what college weekend. We talked about sex, in a roundabout way. "Necking" was okay, "petting" was borderline okay if "you really liked" the boy. "She's quite the girl" was code for having gone "all the way," and such girls were disapproved of.

The pill and the sexual revolution were several years in the future. We did not yet realize how thoroughly we had internalized the social controls protecting us from out-of-wedlock pregnancy, which was still, in the early '50s, a certain disgrace to be feared. Abortion was illegal, and an unwed mother faced social ostracism. Mothers of pregnant girls who could afford it took their daughters to a distant state to a "home for unwed mothers" where the unfortunate girl waited to deliver and immediately place her baby for adoption. Rich parents took girls to Switzerland. We were on our guard: "Men are always thinking about just one thing," we would say darkly to each other. Virginity was valued, a treasure you safeguarded for your future husband. This changed pretty quickly once we had left Farmington, and I doubt that many of my classmates were virgins when they graduated from college.

We had unanswered questions about lesbians; we knew lesbians liked other women rather than men, but not much else. Since the idea of being sexually attracted to a woman seemed odd, we assumed that lesbians were, therefore, peculiar people and misfits. There was only one single-bedded room in the whole school—all the others had two or three beds and some had four. I remember that a solitary, gawky girl named Germaine, a class ahead of mine, was in "the single" for two years. We called her a lesbian, basically because she had no roommate—ironically we discussed "fairies," identifying them on the same irrational grounds we identified poor Germaine. We talked a lot about what "normal" sex might be like and clandestinely circulated a particularly repulsive piece of pornography called "The Nubian Slave," which could have been written to warn young women against losing their virginity. There was no classroom discussion of sex and human reproduction; Mrs. Parminter at Springside had been way ahead of Farmington.

Even though we were, in retrospect, obsessed with boys and acceptance by them, we genuinely valued our friendships with each other, and I still have, more than fifty years later, good friends from those days, women I can telephone after a two-year hiatus and retrieve our former intimacy immediately. There were a number of rituals which encouraged what would now be called "female bonding," as there had been when my mother was at school. Then, romantic friendships between girls were taken for granted. She remembered dancing in the gym on Saturday nights with other girls, and "bunching," secretly throwing bunches of flowers into the room of an older girl you looked up to.

Those customs had disappeared, but we had others. As New Girls, we shared a very unpleasant and unnecessary hazing for a couple of weeks in the late November. The Old Girls refused to smile at us, scowled all the time, and kept saying, "Just you wait until Thanksgiving!" implying that a dreadful punishment for unspecified sins would be meted out then. But it was all a farce: on Thanksgiving Day, which we had to spend at school, the Old Girls suddenly became our friends again. The communal suffering and reprieve cemented our class's relationships with each other. Near the end of the first academic year, there was "wishing on the ring." Each of us had a school ring—mine had been my mother's—and we were supposed to choose an Old Girl to "wish it on." This ceremony was performed in some private place, and many girls became very emotional about it. I thought it creepily too much like an engagement but didn't want to be left out. I asked a senior girl I liked to go through this obligation with me. I don't remember now whether it was Anne Wigglesworth or Anne Sloane, nor do I know what she wished for me, but I was relieved when it was over.

The night before graduation, there was "Singing in the Garden," when all the seniors gathered in a circle, arms linked, to sing school songs, the words written to popular tunes of a bygone time. One was to "Aura Lee" (a song whose tune was later appropriated by Elvis as "Love me Tender") and the chorus went something like this:

Farmington! Farmington!
With thy singing sweet,

Mem'ries softly come and go,
Of a shaded street.

There were others such, familiar melodies with lyrics about love of Farmington. We had sung these songs on various occasions over the three years, and I was pretty cynical about them, so I did not go to the garden the night before my own graduation. My parents were up and staying in the village with Mr. and Mrs. Keep, who had been there as headmaster and headmaster's wife when my mother was there. They kindly invited me to dinner, and I did not mention that "Singing in the Garden" was going on until it was over. When my mother realized that we had missed it, she was horribly disappointed. "Why didn't you tell me?" she kept asking. "I didn't know it was so important to you," I kept answering, and it was true. I hadn't deliberately withheld the information, though a psychiatrist might say otherwise.

On graduation day, we processed through the campus with the traditional daisy chain, wearing our modestly cut, full-skirted white dresses, two by two. I marched with my dear friend and fellow skeptic, Sheila Hollern. Neither of us could get weepy about that daisy chain; it made me sneeze. All I could think was, "Free at last!" I was going to Radcliffe in the fall, along with six of my favorite class-mates, including Sheila. And life was going to begin.

chapter twelve

FIRST TRIP
TO EUROPE

In 1952, the summer after I turned sixteen and had finished my junior year at Farmington, my parents took my brother Walter and me on a month-long trip to Europe. Walt was thirteen. Billy, who was only ten, was deemed too little to appreciate the trip, and he was to be left behind at camp. I think the real reason my parents didn't bring Billy was that five is a more unwieldy number to travel with than four and adds to the expense. They had planned and budgeted the trip carefully: we would go to London, Scotland, Paris, and Switzerland, all places where they had friends. We would stay most of the time with these friends or near them in simple hotels; and very occasionally in a first-class hotel for a night, just to give us a taste of luxury.

The last time Mum and Dad had taken a trip abroad was in 1936, the year I was born, and had parked me, at the age of three months with Muzzie and Yan at Four Winds while they went to the wedding, in England, of one Dad's Princeton roommates. Now, they wanted their children to have some of the experiences they had had themselves when young, and traveling by boat was one of them. Paying for first class was out of the question, and my father disliked intensely the thought of our being, literally, second-class citizens, so they settled on a small, one-class, modestly priced Cunard line ship called the *Media*. (Luckily, it was not *Medea*.) My father's vacation time was limited, so Mum, Walter and I would sail over, he would fly to London and meet us, and he would sail home with us.

My father drove us all, including Billy, to New York. I remember distinctly how my youngest brother looked that day. He was wearing a red baseball cap, a striped polo shirt, brown shorts, and a determinedly stoic expression. He had been officially handed over to my mother's sister Selina, there to see us off and take charge of him; she would install him in Camp La Jeunesse, in Maine, a few days later. I can still see his small, diminishing figure, smiling and waving bravely, as his mother, sister, and brother steamed off. I asked him recently if he remembered the moment, and he said, "How could I forget that? My entire family was sailing away from me across the ocean." It was an awful abandonment, but fortunately one whose scars did not go very deep. My sweet-tempered youngest brother is not given to nursing a grudge.

There were boat rituals my mother happily embraced. Friends had sent bon voyage telegrams and fruit. A passenger list was distributed—I understand that these days, there are no passenger lists, "for security reasons"—and we discovered that Chestnut Hill neighbors were on board, Mr. and Mrs. Dam and daughter Sally, who had been a classmate of mine in Springside days. The Harveys, whom my parents knew, were also on board, with their two sons Bill, who was sixteen, and Jack, two years older, very convenient for Sally and me. (Bill and Sally began a teenage romance which culminated in marriage, after they had both graduated from college. Jack and I were dancing partners, no more.)

The crossing took a leisurely week. My mother and I shared a cabin, and Walter had a smaller one to himself. Every day, under the cabin door, appeared a program of the day's activities to encourage passengers to think there was riotous fun in store. In addition to meals, including "elevenses" on deck (broth and crackers) and an elaborate tea at four, there were games like Bingo and Horse Racing, played with toy horses and dice. I visited the ship's library and found a book called *The Diary of Ann Frank*. I leafed through it and decided it didn't look interesting. So much for my literary judgment at sixteen.

Each evening, when the music started, we "made a party," as 19th century novels put it: the three Dams, four Harveys, and three Foulkes. Sally danced with Bill Harvey and I danced with Jack (sometimes the other way around), the Dams and Harveys danced with each other, and Mr. Dam and Mr. Harvey would each gallantly dance once with my mother. Then, the second night, Denys Smith-Bingham joined the party. He was one of those peripatetic English bachelors, probably somewhere in his forties, with a mustache and sideburns, an Oxbridge accent, and the air of an adventurer. He was a practiced raconteur, and told stories set in India, Africa, and the War. He was a good dancer, as was our graceful mother, and night after night, round and round they went on the little dance floor, tipping when the boat did and laughing as they regained their balance.

Walter and I took a strong and instant dislike to Denys Smith-Bingham. We hated his hyphenated last name and the way he spelled his first, which we considered affected. We hated his British accent, his mustache, and his sideburns. We hated his war stories, which we suspected of being fabricated. Most of all, we hated the admiring way he looked at our mother. How could anyone be attracted to our mother, who was too old for any sort of foolish romance? She was ancient, thirty-six.

"Why can't you just tell him to go away?" we would ask. Mum would respond that it would seem rude, on a small boat, to deny someone permission to join an after-dinner drinking group in the lounge. "Well, you don't have to *dance* with him, do you?" one of us would say, and Mum simply said it was fun dancing with him and there was no harm in it. She was very careful not to dance with him too much, or too close, and to avoid the slightest indication of any impropriety. She knew that the Harveys and the Dams, back in Chestnut Hill, would report all, in detail. In their company, she made frequent references to her sharing a cabin with me.

Once we met my father in London, at the Savoy-Court Hotel (no relation to the grander Savoy) Walter and I continued to tease Mum unmercifully about Mr. Smith-Bingham, to a point where she took us aside and, nearly in tears, begged us, "*Stop it* for heaven's sake! Otherwise, your father will think that something really happened!" We complied, in the interests of family harmony, but for years, when Walter and I were by ourselves, the very words "Smith-Bingham" would set us off into fits of laughter.

The London of 1952 was still recovering from the War and the Blitz; I was shocked to see so many bombed-out buildings not yet rebuilt and deep holes full of rubble. People on the street looked very proper: men in tweeds and bowlers, carrying tightly rolled umbrellas; women in tweeds and stout walking shoes and hats, nearly everyone anglo-saxon—a far cry from the multicultural London of today. My parents adored London and enjoyed showing us the Tower, St. Paul's, Westminster Bridge, and the Changing of the Guard at Buckingham Palace. We went to Harrods, where my mother bought some china which she had sent to the boat, and Harris tweed jackets for me and Walter. "They wear like iron!" she kept saying happily. They did, and I was very tired of mine long before it wore out.

"Uncle Kit" Caslon, a recently retired Admiral in the British Navy, came up from Sussex to meet us and take us to his Club for lunch. He had become a great friend during World War II, when he was for a time in Philadelphia; he and his wife Laurie, with their sons David and Denis, had come to visit us in Northeast Harbor in 1949. Since then, Mum and Laurie had kept up an indefatigable correspondence. We were to stay with them in Littlehampton, Sussex at the end of the trip, but Uncle Kit could not wait that long to see us. After lunch, he took us to the Tate, to look at 19th century English paintings; I kept trying to drift away from them over to the Italian Renaissance paintings, which I considered superior, having been indoctrinated at Farmington by Miss McClennan.

My father was on the board of Philadelphia's Fairmont Park, which had commissioned a statue from the British sculptor Jacob Epstein; Dad had been asked by the board to go and see how the work was coming on, and Epstein kindly invited the rest of us to come too, and to have a drink after the viewing. I was deeply impressed by this visit. Epstein was the first real artist I had ever met, and he looked the part, with his white flyaway hair and slightly rumpled smock-like jacket. His studio looked like my idea of an artist's studio, huge, high-ceilinged, and full of marble in various stages of becoming statues. The corners were full of plaster dust and there were charcoal sketches tacked up here and there. The statue for Fairmont Park was of a woman, three times life-sized, with strong features, straight bangs and straight Cleopatra-type hair to her shoulders. She was to be part of a three-statue installation in bronze, representing Social Consciousness. When we moved to the living room and our hostess appeared, I realized she was the model for one of these statues. My mother murmured to me that she was the mother of Epstein's children and his mistress, but was not his wife—the first woman I had met living such an unconventional life. I was thrilled to be in the midst of what looked like bohemia, and so wonderfully unlike Chestnut Hill.

The conversation turned to our trip, and my father mentioned that we were going that evening to see "South Pacific" with Mary Martin. "You should be taking your children to see John Gielgud, in *As You Like It*, not an American musical," someone said sternly. My father laughed, and said *he* wanted to see "South Pacific", establishing us all as New World provincials among the Old World urban intellectuals.

No matter; my parents called it right. I can't imagine Walter, at thirteen, responding very warmly to Gielgud as Orlando. All of us loved "South Pacific," even though it was an odd thing to be seeing it in London, and I cherish the memory of my father's expression during "There is Nothing Like a Dame." He laughed until tears ran down his cheeks; having served in the Navy, he recognized those sailors. Seeing the recent revival in New York at Lincoln Center brought that first experience back in technicolor.

One somber memory of that evening: there was, at the Epstein house, a skeletal woman introduced as Vicki. I had never seen anyone so thin, and asked my mother afterwards what the matter with her was. My mother, always adept at finding out all about people in a short time, told me that Vicki had been in a concentration camp during the War and had been unable, so far, to get her weight back to anything approaching normal. I had read about concentration camp survivors in *Life* magazine, but had never seen one before; Vicki's face, with deep hollows under the eyes and prominent teeth, haunted me for weeks.

From London we traveled by train to Norfolk to spend three or four days with Lord and Lady Fermoy at Park House in Sandringham. There are a number of details about this visit which have faded. I am sure my mother would have written all about it in letters to her sister Selina, and I would dearly love to have access to these. Unfortunately, during the cleanout of Aunt Selina's house after her death, one of her children, impatient with all the decisions about paper, simply threw them all out. How much of any family's history has been lost this way?

Lord Fermoy had been a classmate of my father's father at St. Paul's School in Concord, N.H. His mother was an American heiress who divorced her English husband and took her twin sons back to the United States, where they grew up. Lord Fermoy was the younger of twins by a few minutes (Wikipedia will tell you he was the older, but this is not so) and his older brother inherited the title when his father, the previous Lord Fermoy, died. But, in one of those Dickensian flukes that belong to real life as well as to novels, the twin brother died suddenly in 1920, and my grandfather's old friend became the Lord, which precipitated his return to England where he assumed his duties in the House of Lords. He had kept in touch with my grandfather until the latter's death in 1917, afterwards with his widow, Muzzie, and, since her death, with my father. His title had not estranged him from his young days in America.

My parents always had a weakness for titles and were eager to make a good impression during this visit. Walter and I were repeatedly briefed on manners during the journey: no interrupting, no talking with mouths full, no roughhousing. Fingernails clean at all times. Walter and I sighed and rolled our eyes. Lord Fermoy met us at King's Lynn and drove us to Sandringham, a property leased from the Crown. He was a tall, white-haired exuberant man in his late sixties who talked non-stop—it would have been hard to interrupt. Park House and the extensive grounds were intimidatingly grand, but the family was democratically warm and welcoming. Lady Fermoy was more than twenty years younger than her husband, which put her close to my mother in age. Like Mum, she was an ardent pianist; they were immediately on a first name basis. There were two daughters, Mary, nearly eighteen, and Frances, going on sixteen. Their last name was Roche, pronounced like the beetle. (Lord Fermoy's name, as distinct from his title, was Maurice—pronounced Morris—Roche.) Mary had made her debut and was at ease in conversation; Frances was still very much a little girl who was awkward talking to strangers. Our first day there, she took me out to the stable to see the pony, in which I politely feigned a nonexistent interest. So our parents decided that even though I was closer in age to Frances, I should spend the most time with Mary.

Mary took me along on a chilly picnic one afternoon with some of her friends, including a couple of young men who had graduated from Eton and were now at Oxford. They spent some time discussing their old school; one of them said, "It's a terrible shame that they have stopped beating the boys." I was horrified. "*Beating* the boys?" I asked. The Etonian graduates explained that yes, while they were there, the older boys routinely beat the younger boys for all sorts of minor infractions. "It's important for discipline," they insisted. I protested that this was nonsense; they kept insisting. It was a moment when the gulf between the U.S. and England yawned very wide.

I never saw either Mary or Frances again, but continued to have news of them from time to time. Only two years later, my mother reported that Frances was marrying a peer twelve years older, a Viscount Althorp, and that she would be "a very great lady." I had a hard time reconciling the sweet but immature Frances I had met with the one being married in Westminster Abbey; the guests included Queen Elizabeth, who was a close friend of Ruth Fermoy's, as well as numerous other royals. My parents did not go to the wedding, but savored the details in the British papers.

My mother kept up a correspondence with Ruth Fermoy over many years and saw her several times on visits to England. In 1967, Ruth wrote that "Frances has been very naughty." What Frances had done was to escape from her husband and "run off" with someone first described to me as a stable groom, then as an aviator, and finally, more prosaically, as a rich commoner, a married man with three children, and the heir to a fortune made from wallpaper in Australia. This was very embarrassing to her mother, who was by then a Lady in Waiting to the Queen Mother. "So Frances bolted," said my mother thoughtfully. I knew about bolting from a Nancy Mitford novel I had read in which there was a character called "The Bolter." It was as difficult for me to imagine Frances in this role as it had been to see her as a bride in Westminster Abbey.

In an ensuing court battle, Frances lost the custody of her two younger children to her husband. Ruth Fermoy, who believed firmly in the indissolubility of marriage, testified against her daughter's fitness as a mother. I report this in such detail because one of Frances's children was Diana, later Princess of Wales. Sadly, Ruth and her daughter Frances were never reconciled; now both are dead and it is too late. I know that Mary, who has been twice divorced, is still alive, as I saw not long ago an advertisement for a book she had written about her father. Some day, I will send for it.

After a few days, we descended to London by train and, thanks to the generosity of Lady Fermoy and my mother's talent for making friends, were able to use the

Fermoy's town house on Wilton Crescent as a place to rest and re-pack before taking a night train to Invergordon, Scotland. There, we stayed with more friends, the Mathesons, who had a sheep farm. They had a bouncy Welsh cairn which was an astonishing shade of pink. Alec Matheson explained that the dog was normally gray, but had accidentally fallen into the sheep dip used to prevent mites, and changed color. "He'll return to gray, eventually," said Mrs. Matheson.

Every morning during our stay, little Lucy Matheson, aged five, brought "early morning tea" to me and to my parents, knocking softly at the door before opening it and slipping in to put a precariously jiggling cup held in two small hands on the night table. Our first morning, she took me to see the pony. I was just as uninterested in this one as in the last, but Lucy was so enthusiastic about it that, again, I pretended enchantment.

We had been prepared for cold and rain, but the weather was uncharacteristically warm and sunny. Mrs. Matheson said she had worn a cotton dress only three times that summer, the three days we were with them. The Mathesons took advantage of the fine weather to drive us all around the Scottish countryside visiting castles and the sites of battles; what I remember best are the one-lane roads with occasional pull-outs in case of a car came head to head from the opposite direction. The car closest to a pull-out backed up into it and allowed the other car to pass. These roads wound through rolling, treeless moors covered with heather which made me think of *Wuthering Heights* and made my father say "Now I see why Alan Breck, in *Kidnapped*, had to lie down in the heather to avoid being seen." Thirty-four years later, on the first trip in Scotland I'd had since 1952, I was astonished to find so much landscape virtually unchanged. The one-lane roads through the heathered moors were still there and we still had to back up to a pullout to avoid headlong collision with someone coming the other way.

FROM SCOTLAND, WE returned to London and flew to Geneva. This was my first flight ever. The roaring as we took off frightened me, and like a small child, I held my mother's reassuring hand. We stayed a couple of nights in the Beau Rivage Hotel, a first-class interlude which I thoroughly enjoyed. I reveled in having a room to myself, breakfast in bed with real coffee, not the bitter chicory of the Savoy Court. "My daughter loves luxury," my father observed ruefully, but he took undisguised pleasure in offering this treat to his family.

Geneva's streets were jammed with bicycles ridden by people who used them as their primary mode of transportation. I remember the way they obeyed traffic lights, like cars—I was used to riding a bike in places where two-wheeled traffic was cut a lot of slack. I remember also the swimming beach by the lake. I was very interested in the bathing suits worn by both women and men, which were noticeably skimpier than those in the U.S., and by what they revealed. I discovered that, even in my extremely modest one-piece suit, I attracted glances from men, and, when my parents were not around, I looked back at them and made eye contact. Was this risky? I don't think so. Evidently, European women enjoyed being looked at, and European men enjoyed the freedom to look.

From Geneva, we took a cog railway up to a mountain village called Champéry, where Robert and Irma Ador, more friends of my parents', spent their summers. Irma, as a young widow, had spent the war years in Philadelphia, and she and my mother had become very close; Irma was able to speak French with Mum, a comfort in her early days in a foreign country. The ride up the mountain was breathtaking; the scenery looked exactly like the illustrations in my well-read copy of *Heidi*: snow-capped peaks, lush green meadows full of wild flowers, classic wooden chalets with sharply peaked roofs weighted down with stones, herds of cattle, and, occasionally, women and little girls in dirndls. I couldn't believe it was all real.

The Adors met us at the train station. My parents were meeting Robert, her second husband, for the first time, and liked him immediately. Robert and Irma, who became lifelong friends to my parents, were entirely at home in English, a good thing since my father's French, like mine, was basic, and Walter's was non-existent. They had a little boy, Jean-Pierre, four years old and irresistible in lederhosen who spoke only French, the first such child I had met, and the first with a hyphenated first name. How was it possible for him to rattle off a language I still found so sticky on my tongue?

The Adors' summer chalet was too small to accommodate a visiting family of four, and we stayed nearby, in an immaculate and friendly small hotel. The food there, and at the Adors, seemed sublime after English food. My father was enchanted by the beauty of the Alpine surroundings, the invigorating mountain air, the warm welcome of the Ador family, and the cuisine. In the newspapers, he read about a heat wave in Paris, which was to be our next stop. Daddy always hated heat, and he began musing about canceling Paris altogether and going straight back to England, where we were to finish our trip with a visit to the Caslons in Sussex. He always felt at home in England. Walter and I were appalled at the prospect of skipping Paris, and began singing, loudly, and often, "The Last Time I Saw Paris," (a favorite of my father's):

The last time I saw Paris,
Her trees were decked for spring,
And lovers met beneath those trees,
And birds found songs to sing.
I dodged the same old taxicabs
That I had dodged for years,
The chorus of their squeaky horns
Was music to my ears.
The last time I saw Paris,
Her heart was young and gay,
No matter how they change her,
I'll remember her that way.

Whether we wore him down or whether it was too much trouble to change all the arrangements I don't know, but in the end, we did go to Paris on schedule.

In Paris, we stayed at a small hotel off the Rue de Rivoli, the Oxford et Cambridge, a name which says much. I remember cramped rooms, a lot of dark red walls and upholstery, surly personnel, and my mother, with her superior French, doing most of the negotiating, which bothered Dad. He was not fond of French breakfasts, which consisted of carefully rationed bread (sometimes croissants), butter, jam, and café au lait, and often said, "I don't know what keeps the French going until lunch. Maybe it's the milk." One morning, before my mother was down, he tried to order bacon and eggs, in his halting French, and when the waiter haughtily refused to understand, he exploded, insofar as he was able to do this in French, and finally got results. What eventually appeared was more like an omelet than scrambled eggs and the bacon was fried ham; nevertheless, it was a significant victory.

Despite the rudeness of waiters, I loved almost everything about Paris, and still do. I fell for all the things first-time visitors fall for: the sidewalk cafés, the arcades of the rue de Rivoli and the stylish shop windows, the bookstalls along the Seine, the Tuileries gardens with the children sailing boats in the ponds. Women still dressed to go out then, in suits, gloves, and high heels, and just walking around the more fashionable streets was like being part of a daily Easter Parade. We went up to Montmartre one evening and stood in the doorway of a small cabaret too jammed for us to enter, listening to a chanteuse singing "Matelot" in a throaty voice—

Il y a dans chaque port
Une fille qui t'adore—

—and one about the Seine which ended *"Car la Seine a une amante, et Paris dors dans son lit."* An indelible quarter hour.

A highlight was a day at Longchamps, where my mother, not a habitué of racetracks, bet on a horse chosen largely by the color of the jockey's silks, and, against the odds, won a large number of francs, enough to take us all to dinner at an expensive Russian restaurant called Dinarzhade. We ate by candlelight in an enclosed garden whose walls were covered with ivy while Russian violinists played gypsy music. I thought Paris was the most wonderfully sophisticated place I could imagine. I became on the spot an American cliché.

Another highlight was the day Bill White and his Swedish wife Gertrud (pronounced "Yertrud") took me to Chartres, without my parents. Traveling with my parents for several weeks without my usual avenues of escape had begun to be trying for us all, and the Whites, who were visiting Paris at the same time, offered to remove me for a day. We went by train, and the Whites treated me like an equal, drew me out with non-patronizing questions, and appeared genuinely interested in the answers. We spent the day savoring that magnificent cathedral and its stunning stained-glass windows, so much more dazzling in real life than on Miss McClennan's slides. The Whites joined the ranks of favorite-friends-of-my-parents. In the future, I was always happy to see them and they me, and I cherish a blue crystal bowl which Gertrud brought back from a trip to Sweden as a wedding present for us, three years later. She didn't entrust it to her checked luggage but held it in her lap all the way across the Atlantic. I have been back several times to Chartres since then, and while there, I always think of that initial visit and the kindness of the Whites.

From Paris, we returned to England and went to Littlehampton, on the Sussex coast, to visit the Caslon family. Their modest house, like that of the Adors, being too small for all of us, they had found a nearby hotel called the White Jade. I have a vivid memory of my mother coming into the room Walter and I shared early one morning with a telegram in her hand and tears in her eyes. " It's from Brownie," she said. (This was Mr. Brownell's nickname.) "Gwladys has died." Mum had known before leaving that Gwladys was ill with cancer but had prayed hard for her recovery. Of all her many friends, Gwladys was the one who shared most completely her love of music—they had often played together piano music written for four hands—her sense of humor, and of course the memories of the War years as Navy wives in Cape May, the "dismal spit." Her loss was painful. More painful still was her understanding of what it would mean for Gwladys's four children to be motherless. Two, Larry and

Ruggles were in their teens, Martha was ten and Freddie only six. In later years, my mother often referred to Gwladys's death as an example of why it is necessary to have regular check-ups, a lesson that I internalized. She was convinced that had the cancer been diagnosed sooner, Gwladys could have been saved.

In order not to let her grief blight our enjoyment of the last ten days of the trip, she did not dwell on it, but I knew it was always underneath whatever we did. She told the Caslons and talked a little about her old friend, but left it at that. She didn't want to spoil her own enjoyment either, and she especially loved two events that the Caslons had arranged.

One was an outing to the Goodwood Races, near Chichester, in West Sussex. The racecourse was on the estate of the Earl of March, whose castle was part of the landscape but not open to the public. Goodwood was a very social event, comparable to Ascot; everyone dressed up for it and a sport equal to the racing itself was celebrity-spotting. My parents had a glimpse of Princess Margaret, which delighted them. She was pointed out to me, and I pretended indifference, in reaction to my parents, but once home, I boasted about having seen her.

The other memorable event from the Caslon visit was a ball in Arundel Castle. The Duke of Arundel gave—and for all I know, the present Duke still gives—an annual summer ball for the gentry and people of note in Sussex. We had been forewarned, so Mum and I had brought long dresses and my father his dinner jacket (he always used this phrase instead of "tuxedo.") Walter was too young to own evening wear, so he wore a blue blazer, white shirt and tie. Uncle Kit and Aunt Laurie were invited because of his having served as an Admiral in the Queen's Navy. I was initially disappointed that there was no cutting in on the dance floor, as at home; the custom was to dance only with members of one's own party, unless formally introduced to a potential dancing partner, which did not happen. (I felt as though I were in a Jane Austen novel.) I don't remember the Caslons knowing very many people. At least I had David and Denis Caslon to dance with, as well as Uncle Kit and my father, who didn't count. David was about 20, and already at Oxford, and Denis was 18. I'd known them first when the family came to visit us in Northeast Harbor four years earlier and, even though we were older, we felt like old friends.

The Queen herself was to attend the ball, and the Caslons and my parents tried, discreetly, to spot her in the crowd. No luck, until my mother made a visit to the ladies' room, and on her way in was suddenly face to face with Queen Elizabeth coming out, flanked by two ladies-in-waiting. As Mum tells it, she stopped and made a deep curtsy, which the Queen graciously acknowledged with a royal nod. My mother tended, always, to make frequent trips to the ladies' room, but "this time," said my father, "it really paid off." They both loved the story of meeting the Queen at the loo, and repeated it often. Now that they are both gone, I find myself telling it, sixty years later.

chapter thirteen

RADCLIFFE AT LAST

onsidering how important my Radcliffe years were
to me, it is surprising that I cannot remember by
what means of transportation I arrived in Cambridge in September, 1953. I don't think my mother drove
me; it was a long way from Philadelphia and she was used
to the convenience of simply putting me on the train for
West Hartford. I may have taken the train to Boston in
the company of Joanie Mathieson, my good friend from
both Springside and Farmington. What I do remember
is the exhilarating feeling of new-found freedom and a
sense of the world opening wide. I immediately loved
everything about Radcliffe: the semi-urban setting and
the ten-minute MTA ride to Boston, the coeducational
classes, the chance to meet and talk to young women

and men whose backgrounds and experiences were very different from mine, and, finally, the liberation from the restrictions at Farmington. In Cambridge, I could breathe.

How did I happen to end up at a place where I felt so at home? Some of it was dumb luck. My parents had always promised me I could choose my college, although I am sure they privately retained veto power. It was Mr. Johnson, the headmaster of Farmington, who first got me and several of my friends interested in applying to Radcliffe, which sounded perfect to me, and of course I was influenced by its being the choice of so many classmates I liked. My conscientious mother had taken me on a college visiting tour. She let me share the driving, as I'd had my license for a year. The first stop was Bryn Mawr, twenty minutes from Chestnut Hill, and my parents' first choice for me. ("You'd live in a dormitory, and we wouldn't bother you." I suspected otherwise and ruled it out.) Then up to Wellesley, where Mum was impressed by the music department, and Wellesley became her second choice for me. Her third was Vassar, which I rejected as it was too popular with Farmington girls. All of these were women's colleges, and I wanted coeducation. Bill's presence at Harvard was definitely a plus, but not the deciding factor he likes to think it was.

My interview at Radcliffe has become a family legend. Dean Elliott, who was Dean of Admissions, asked me a standard question, "What makes you want to come to Radcliffe?" Naively confident, I answered "I hear you have an excellent domestic science program." I had been denied domestic science at Farmington, having been pigeonholed as Academic, and had yearned after practical knowledge. I can't for the life of me think how or where I had picked up the idea that Radcliffe offered domestic science. Dean Elliott was horrified and contemptuous. "Domestic science!" she spat out. "We have no domestic science here. Our curriculum is *Harvard's!*" Properly cowed, I hastily babbled out other reasons I wanted to come to Radcliffe—the superb education, the diversity of the student body (diverse for 1953), the cultural opportunities, etc. etc.—but it was a miracle that I was accepted.

My parents were suspicious of Radcliffe; it was the era of the McCarthy hearings, and several Harvard professors had been interrogated about their patriotism. "I'm afraid you might become a Communist," said Daddy. His fears were groundless; I was pretty apolitical. My parents eventually reassured themselves with the knowledge that "so many nice girls from Farmington are going," and allowed me to go north without further complaint. That I took for granted—worse, felt *entitled to*—the opportunity to go to college, and to a college of my own choosing, paid for by my parents, is one of many attitudes I now blush to recall. Later, one time when my mother was visiting me at Radcliffe, she burst out "Oh, Lou, I so envy you this wonderful college life!" and I felt a sharp pang of regret for her. She would have reveled in it, as I did. Her parents could have afforded it, but, as I mentioned earlier, they saw no point in higher education for ladies—in fact, they thought of it as a liability—and Mum was an obedient daughter.

I WAS ASSIGNED to Cabot Hall, one of eight brick buildings around a grassy quadrangle, two to a side. Each dorm had girls from all four classes, which encouraged us to make friends in other years. (At Harvard, all freshmen were in houses in the Yard.) There were fewer than 1,000 girls in all on campus, making the ratio with Harvard men, including those in graduate schools, reportedly 10 to 1. At the time, this figure made us regard Cambridge as a heaven of dating possibilities. That there were disadvantages to being so outnumbered did not occur to me until long after I had graduated.

At that time, most of the rooms in the dorms were singles, and the only ones for two were called "economy doubles." They were the same size as the singles, but furnished with two desks, two chests of drawers, and bunk beds. Suzannah Ryan, a Farmington friend from New York, and I had signed up for an economy double, not because our parents had asked us to economize but because we were used to having roommates at Farmington, and we both thought we'd feel lonely in a single. Despite the close quarters, we got on well, but we did feel pretty cramped by all that furniture. When one of us wanted to get into the shared closet, the other had to stand in the hall or climb onto the lower bunk. At the end of freshman year, we signed up for two singles near each other, with a sigh of relief.

We need not have feared loneliness. For one thing, there were seven of us in all who went to Radcliffe from Farmington. Besides Joanie, Suzannah, and me, there were Sheila Hollern, Norah Robinson, Ann Taylor, and Mary Lenore Blair, all of whom I had been close to. Several girls I knew from Philadelphia were also in our class, including Louise Purves from Miss Zara and Springside days, and Bobbie Lingelbach from violin lessons. For another, there was a lounge on each floor that served as a social center in which there were always several lively conversations going on. Cabot Hall gave me at least two lifelong friends, Lucia Stein and the late Peggy Polk. And for a third, the college arranged many activities designed to introduce freshmen to each other, as well as co-ed mixers with Harvard boys known as "Jolly-ups," a name inflicted on these gatherings in an earlier era and now the object of much derision. The first week, our photographs were taken for a booklet called the "Freshman Register," designed to help us and our housemothers recognize each other. The rumor went round that Harvard freshmen pored over these photos before the Jolly-ups, identifying those girls they'd most like to meet.

Most of us got from The Radcliffe Quad to Harvard Yard, where most of our classes took place, by bicycle, a ten-minute journey. The Yard was bigger than our Quad and altogether more redolent of history. It was always full of students in groups of twos and threes, crossing paths, greeting each other, pausing to chat, running at the last minute to get to class on time. Although the scene is similar now, the look is very different: there was a dress code in the '50s which obliged young men to wear coats and ties to classes, and young women to wear skirts. We wore either knee socks or tights—only on snow days were pants permitted. No denim anywhere.

Across Massachusetts Avenue from the Yard is Harvard Square, which is not a "square" at all, but a confluence of streets with an MTA subway station at the point of convergence. Bookstores abounded in that era—along Mass Ave., opposite one side of the Yard, and on side streets. There was Schoenhof's, specializing in foreign-language books, and the Mandrake, owned and run by a Mr. Rosen, who in seconds could put his hand on any title you asked him about, no matter how esoteric. I absorbed a lot about what I ought to read to consider myself educated just by looking in bookstore windows. One day, I thought, I would dig into Joyce's *Ulysses* with the help of a guide to it, and into Proust's *Remembrance of Things Past* in French. The Harvard Cooperative, known as the Coop, was on the corner of Massachusetts and Brattle. Students bought most textbooks at the Coop, and carried them around in dark green drawstring bags slung over one shoulder, the badge of belonging.

Once those mixers, and our classes, had done their work, we Radcliffe women fell into a coeducational social life which was, above all, fun. There were ad hoc gatherings at Cronin's, a popular bar-restaurant, with its high-backed booths; parties in the Harvard dorms and clubs; Saturday breakfasts at Hayes-Bickford in the Square, all characterized by nonstop conversation punctuated by laughter.

I have said that I felt at home in Cambridge, which is true. It is also true that many of my classmates, male and female, seemed far more intellectually sophisticated than I and much brighter, and I suffered from "imposter syndrome": I believed that I did not deserve to be at Harvard and that being accepted had been a clerical error. Like many young people who go to competitive colleges, I underwent a huge psychological readjustment from being someone who had good grades with a minimum of effort to being someone who had to scramble for a B. Still, although I felt out of my depth at times—not in Fine Arts 13, thanks to Miss McClennan—mostly I felt I'd been waiting all my life to get to this blessed spot where people liked discussing literature and ideas, out of class as well as in. (Were the *Iliad* and the *Odyssey* the work of one author, or two, or several? What is happening to the American Labor movement? How free is the will?) I look back on my first two years there as a time when my heart was light and everything was still ahead. Halcyon days.

My courses were exciting, and demanding far beyond anything I'd had before. The General Education program that had been put into place after the end of World War II was required of all undergraduates. It had been deliberately designed to humanize students so fully that we would never again engage in a world war. Each of three areas, Humanities, Social Sciences, and Natural Sciences (known as "Hum", "Soc. Sci.," and "Nat. Sci." offered five or six full-year broadly based lecture courses; students were required to take one in each area some time during the freshman and sophomore years. These would give us the intellectual underpinnings for more advanced study. The Gen. Ed. courses met three times a week for an hour, with a fourth hour for a small group section led by a graduate student. We got many more hours of instruction for our parents' money than students do today. Not only were there more hours a week per course, there were more weeks per semester. "Fall" went from September, after Labor Day, until mid-January; Reading period and exams took up the second half of January, and "Spring" began in February after a very short break, and went through mid-May, followed by another reading period—much of it spent on the banks of the Charles River welcoming the spring sun—and final exams in late May and early June. The two-week reading period gave us the chance to do all the work we had failed to do earlier, being too busy socializing at Cronin's and at Hayes-Bickford, and engaging in long philosophical conversations in the dorm lounge.

That first year, I remember with special pleasure "Hum. 2, Epic and Novel." The first semester, Epic, was taught by John Finlay, a famously erudite and charismatic professor who used no notes. He was a gifted performer; he would stride around the stage carrying his microphone, swishing the cord out of his way like a lion tamer with a whip, bringing the *Iliad*, the *Odyssey* and the *Aeneid* to life. The brilliant verse translations of Robert Fitzgerald, Richmond Lattimore, and Robert Fagles were still in the future, but even working with relatively leaden prose translations, Finlay had me spellbound. I believed utterly in the relevance and importance of Achilles, Hector, Odysseus, Menelaus and Helen of Troy, Dido and Aeneas and the rest. They *mattered.* Many years later, I would read that Finlay had fallen victim to Alzheimer's and would wince at the irony.

I.A. Richards gave the Novel half of the course, which began with *Don Quixote.* (Richards pronounced it in the British manner, *Don Quicks-ot.*) The other novels I remember reading were *Manon Lescaut* and *The Sorrows of Young Werther* (both short, probably chosen to give us a breather), *War and Peace,* and Dostoevsky's *The Possessed,* though there must have been more. I respected Richards but it was Finlay's showmanship which hooked me, hooked us all.

For my Gen. Ed. Nat. Sci. course, I chose the one with the reputation for being geared to humanities majors, Nat. Sci. 3, which was a history of science course taught by I.B. Cohen. It was supposed to be the easiest Nat. Sci., but with my limited background in science and math, it was plenty hard. It included a long section on physics, which was particularly difficult for me. I got through it by diligent memorizing and coaching by a more science-minded new friend in the dorm who was two years older, Paula Omansky. She had gone to the elite Boston Latin, a highly selective public school, and was destined to be in the first class of women admitted to Harvard Law School a few years later. (Even later, she became a distinguished labor lawyer, much honored for her work.)

The only thorn on the rose was Gen. Ed. AHF, a fifth course required of all freshmen and taught by a grad student. (What the AHF stood for is anyone's guess.) This was a weekly expository writing course. Mary Lenore Blair and I were in a section taught by Max Bluestone, who later became a well-known professor of English Renaissance literature at the University of Massachusetts. We were convinced that his mission that year was to show freshmen how much they still had to learn—particularly ones who had been to private schools. The first assignment was to write an analysis of a chapter in Philip Wylie's *Generation of Vipers*. I thought Wylie's criticism of the American "Mom" was unduly harsh and said so. For the first time in my life, I had a D, which shook me to the core, even though Mary Lenore had the same grade. I had always been told I wrote well, and so had she. Max Bluestone was probably right in his assessment that my argument was emotional rather than logical, but I was upset and resentful. We wrote an essay a week, and my grades gradually improved, as did Mary Lenore's, rising to B+ and A-, but we always thought that the upward curve did not represent real progress—it was intended to demonstrate how much Max had taught us. *We* didn't think our writing was very different at the end of the year. Fortunately for my ego, I did very well in a creative writing course given by a young Lecturer named Friedman. He gave me my only straight-A of the year, which encouraged me in my dreams of becoming a writer.

What about my non-academic life? For two years, I sang alto with the Radcliffe Choral Society, directed by G. Wallace Woodworth, "Woody," which was an enormous source of pleasure; singing Bach's B-minor mass and the Brahms Requiem gave me goosebumps. My sophomore year, with Lucia and Peggy, I sold ads to local businesses for the literary magazine, the *Harvard Advocate*—Radcliffe girls could not have editorial positions, but as a reward for doing scut work, we were invited to the parties, where we could drink martinis and rub elbows with some of the famous writers who came to read at Harvard, like Edith Sitwell. I also had a small part in a Poet's Theater play, "The Gospel Witch," as one of several nasty little girls falsely accusing an innocent housewife.

DURING MY FRESHMAN year, I dated a number of young men besides Bill—"dating" then meant only going out for dinner, to a concert, to a football game, to the movies, or just a cup of coffee in Hayes Bick. Some boys were potential romantic interests, some were only friends. (Well, maybe a little innocent flirting went on.) It was a heady time, coming as it did after the nunnery of Farmington. But after the summer of 1954, I came back for sophomore year engaged to Bill, although the official announcement in the Philadelphia papers, the party, and the ring did not follow until the weekend after Thanksgiving. After that, when boys asked me out, which they did, I would explain that I was already committed to someone. I was eighteen and felt that I was capable of a truly adult decision—which I was decidedly not.

We planned to be married in June, after Bill graduated. I would go with Bill to wherever his ROTC assignment took him, hoping to get back to Radcliffe at some point. I had come to college thinking vaguely, as so many Farmington girls did, that I would get married after a couple of years, but in my freshman year I had fallen in love with learning; I was determined to finish my undergraduate education, recognizing that it might not be at Radcliffe.

One had to declare a major at the start of sophomore year, and I had never doubted that English would be mine. My father had majored in English literature at Princeton, which influenced me. Several of my friends chose to major in History and Literature, a demanding double major which I considered and then rejected, since it would have left me no time for creative writing courses (One could not major in creative writing; otherwise, that might have been my choice.) Required for majors was an overview of British literature; our textbook was the hefty two-volume *Major British Writers*, which is still on a shelf in my study, along with other college texts. We began with *Beowulf* in translation, went on to some of the *Canterbury Tales* in Middle English, spent a long time in the English Renaissance, including a lot of Spenser's *Faerie Queen* and a couple of Shakespeare's plays, and, to wind up the first semester, several books of Milton's *Paradise Lost*. Those were the highlights—many less "major" writers were touched on, too. Each literary-historical period was taught by a different professor; we were exposed to writers (and teachers) we might want to return to in more depth in junior year. It was a big lecture course, and while the effort to expose us to the broad sweep was laudable, it was not especially stimulating. There was surely a weekly section for discussion, but I have no recollection of it. We read few women writers; only George Eliot and the Brontës were considered worthy of the canon. Nor were there any women lecturers. At the time, I accepted the status quo, unquestioningly, and now wonder how I could have been so ... unquestioning.

The English History survey I took the same year was enormously exciting. It was taught by David Owen, another of those electrifying teachers who, like John Finlay, could hold a large group of students spellbound. I took copious notes, believed every word he said, and only years later realized that there was no such thing, strictly speaking, as "English history," only interpretations of it, and that I'd had a wonderful course in English History According to David Owen. This is not a reproof—he shaped and colored the large body of information in ways that made it fascinating to us.

The course that meant the most to me, though, was the creative writing seminar, fiction and poetry, taught by Archibald MacLeish. MacLeish was the Boylston Professor of Rhetoric and Composition. This honor included the right to tether a cow on the Cambridge common, a right not invoked for two hundred years. Although not remembered much now, MacLeish was at the time a well-considered poet and occasional playwright. (One of his plays, *J.B.*, based on the Book of Job, was produced in New York the spring of that year.) The MacLeish seminar, a full-year course, met twice a week from four to six p.m. MacLeish accepted only twelve students, usually juniors and seniors, and I was never sure why he had accepted me; it may have been because I'd had a piece of light verse published in *The New Yorker* the year before. I was the only sophomore and the only girl in the class, so intimidated that I did not open my mouth for weeks. At each meeting, one or two people were "up" and read their work to the others, who then discussed what they had heard, so critically and so confidently, as it seemed to me, with many references to books I had not read or even heard of, that I was terrified of my first turn, scheduled for the middle of the semester. From what the others wrote, I had the impression that almost everyone else was either Jewish or a lapsed Catholic and suffering from various intriguing forms of guilt. Though a WASP, I, too, had plenty of guilt, but mine seemed to me of a less interesting variety.

MacLeish was an excellent moderator, always managing to elicit at least some favorable comments, and leading the group to both a reasoned evaluation of what they had heard and to concrete suggestions for revision. Luckily, my first story, "The End of the War," met with favor, and MacLeish even encouraged me to try and publish it. (I was never able to, and have been rewriting the story at intervals all my life.) I was still awed by the superior literary knowledge of the others, but at least felt accepted by the class, if not as a full equal.

One young man, Leo, developed a crush on me and told a classmate, "I can't decide if I'm in love with her or not." I said tartly to the boy who reported this to me, "It doesn't matter if he is or isn't—I'm engaged to be married." After that, Leo decided that he was *definitely* in love with me—I was so safe!—and sighed longingly at me across the seminar table for a few weeks.

I learned an enormous amount both from MacLeish and from my classmates about how to *think* about literature and writing; what kinds of questions to consider, and to ask; and also—although this realization came much later, when I became a teacher myself—how to teach in a way that involved students actively in their own learning.

Several times, Macleish invited us to his house to meet real writers. I remember an evening with John Crowe Ransome when he read "Bells for John Whiteside's Daughter," a poignant poem about a child who died, and a picnic in the spring at the MacLeish farm where we met Eric Bentley, who had recently translated Brecht's *Threepenny Opera*. We were inspired to think that we, too, might be one day among the elect. Some of my MacLeish classmates did achieve distinction as scholars (Stephen Booth), poets (Alan Grossman, who was also a Brandeis professor), editors (Rob Cowley), and writers (Peter Sourian, a novelist who taught writing at Bard). However, in one of the individual conferences he held at intervals, he told me I was *hors concours*—"not allowed to compete, ineligible because of superiority" according to one of my French dictionaries. I have never known exactly what he meant: since I was clearly not in the "superiority" category, did he mean that he expected me to settle down and raise a family and forget about a career of any kind? Or did he mean I lacked the drive, ambition, and talent of the men? I will never know—but his prophecy was correct in that I never became a professional writer, although I later published a couple of short stories, a few articles about teaching, and a couple of book reviews.

I also took, in the fall, a course in the civilizations of China and Japan, familiarly known as "Rice Paddies," taught jointly by Reischauer and Fairbank. Although the two lecturers were excellent, this was a misstep. It was a "fifth course" for me—only four were required—and the amount of material was so vast I simply could not master it. I did come away with a tremendous respect for the antiquity and scope of Far Eastern history and culture. After the first few months of freshman year, my grades had improved, but after barely getting a C for the fall semester of Rice Paddies, I did not sign up for the spring half.

Knowing I would not be back for junior year affected my spring course choices. I figured that some of the requirements most people got out of the way during the first two years might change. I went on with the MacLeish seminar, the British History course, and English 10, but decided not to get the basic Gen Ed. Soc. Sci out of the way as who knew? The administration might decide to abolish that requirement. Instead, I seized on a couple of courses that I figured might disappear in my absence. One of them was "Folksong and Balladry," given by my freshman year creative writing teacher, Al Friedman, which turned out to be surprisingly serious and very illuminating. Another was a graduate-level course in modern poetry (Yeats, Pound, Eliot, Auden, Dylan Thomas, Marianne Moore) with Edwin Honig. There were only 18 or so in the class, several of them graduate students, so there was, as in the MacLeish class, interaction between teacher and students. During the student protests of the late '60s and early '70s, when one of the students' complaints was the impersonality of large lecture courses, I felt grateful I'd been able to take one or two small classes each year.

Bill and I were to be married in June, and there is a lot about the spring semester that has gone down the memory hole. I do remember wondering how could I bear to leave this intellectual feast behind. This was, increasingly, a question that bothered me as our wedding date drew closer. My father's promise to pay for the rest of my undergraduate education comforted me, and, as it turned out, I was able to return in the fall of 1958, when Bill entered Harvard Business School. By then, we were the parents of a one-year-old son, living in an apartment in North Cambridge, and the college experience of those last two years was quite different from those first two.

THE WEDDING
CERTIFICATE

L ike my mother before me, I was married at 19, and
had a story to tell about the aftermath of the wedding. Hers involved a suitcase left by the side of the
road and managed to make the Philadelphia papers. Mine
involved almost missing the plane that was to take Bill
and me to Barcelona for the start of our honeymoon—
hardly newsworthy, though of moment to us.

In November 1934, following the reception at her parents' house, "Red Roof," in Wawa, a large, traditional affair
with all the usual cake-cutting, toasts, bouquet throwing
and so on, Mum and my father were en route to New York,

driven by Arthur, her parents' long-time trusted chauffeur. After a night at the Plaza Hotel, they were to take a boat to Nassau for their honeymoon. My parents realized about halfway to New York that the car was full of rice that had been thrown at them and asked Arthur to stop the car so that they could brush it out. They did not want to look like obvious newlyweds when they arrived at the Plaza and be subjected to knowing smiles from the staff.

Only on arriving at the hotel did my mother realize that her most important suitcase had been left by the side of the road while the rice was cleaned out. "Most important" because it contained not only the nicest clothes in her trousseau, including a hand-embroidered wedding-night-gown, but also a family heirloom opal pin, passed down from bride to bride—and, crucially, her diaphragm, which had recently become legal. From a phone booth in the next town, she telephoned her parents, who telephoned the highway patrol, and the suitcase was quickly recovered, turned in by an honest soul who happened to notice it as he drove by. Everything was still in it. But there was not time for it to reach New York before the boat sailed, and my mother had to wait until the return from Nassau to have it in her hands.

Someone gave the story to the *Philadelphia Inquirer* and in the memorabilia from my parents' house is a yellowed clipping from the front page with an unflattering photo of Mum in a cloche hat and the headline, "Bride's Suitcase Left on Highway." (It must have been a slow news day.) The article did not say anything about the nightgown or the diaphragm but did mention the opal pin. "Opals are traditionally unlucky," Mum always said when telling the story, "but this one has the reputation of being lucky."

Danny, her mother, had never discussed sex with her daughter, who had learned the fundamentals of reproduction from reading, from married older cousins, and by keeping her ears open. Hearing about the lost suitcase, Danny decided that the time had come for communication with her daughter about family planning, and when Arthur returned to Red Roof, she sent him right back up to New York with a package containing her own rudimentary birth-control apparatus, a kind of douche-bag, along with a note explaining how to use it. My father probably went out and bought some "protection," but I wasn't told that.

Our wedding story is not as dramatic.

When Bill and I married in 1955, I was better prepared; Mum had reacted against her own mother's reticence and ignorance by being open about sex, and at times embarrassingly forthright. But I was no less innocent. Driving to the church with my father, I had been so terrified I could not utter a word. I was not afraid of anything that might happen on the wedding night but feared for my whole future. I was in love with Bill, but marriage was a heart-stopping commitment. I felt that I was on a high diving board with no guarantee of what would happen when I hit the water, and that the only way to find out was hold my nose and jump. I counted on Bill's being a grown-up, an older man at twenty-two who would figure out our lives. The wedding and the reception remain a blur.

In our experience, weddings in those days were not as elaborate as they are now. In Philadelphia, the Protestant Episcopal versions usually began at four in the afternoon with a church ceremony and were followed by a glorified afternoon tea. Our reception was at Beechen Green, and two Scots in kilts piped in the guests. There was an array of tea-sandwiches and petits-fours on tables under a tent on the lawn. Maybe there was cold chicken, maybe salmon. Iced tea and soft drinks were served at first, for the receiving line, then mixed drinks at 5, and then champagne. There was a traditional wedding cake—that's where the champagne fit in—and a traditional cake-cutting. There are photographs to prove it. But no real dinner, except for the bridal party, who sat around the dining room table at six o'clock and feasted while the other guests milled about and socialized under the tent. I ate almost nothing. There must have been a small combo, as I remember dancing on the terrace, ceremonially, with my father and then Bill, to "Shall We Dance?" from *The King and I*, while relatives and friends beamed at us approvingly.

In the basement recreation room, tidied up for the occasion, were all the wedding presents on long tables, on display, with the cards of those who sent them. This gauche custom, fortunately, has disappeared.

It was a very hot and sticky June day and there was no air-conditioning in the church or at home, as was normal. I was wearing my mother's long-sleeved wedding dress in ivory satin, the material originally chosen for her November ceremony. It had been remodeled for me, each fitting requiring a narrower waist, as I lost weight steadily during the month before the wedding. I wore a Wood family lace veil ("something borrowed") and the lucky opal ("something blue" or approximately). Bill, like his ushers had on a morning coat, wing collar and ascot, and both of us remember perspiring a lot. The nine bridesmaids—nine!—were cooler, in white, short-sleeved organdy dresses with wide pale blue dropped-waist sashes tied in a big bow in back. I had chosen them from a photograph Mum sent to me, showing them from the back, the picturesque angle. They were universally unflattering in front, and I have it on good authority that most went within a week to Goodwill Industries or a church Opportunity Shop.

At six, Bill and I were sent upstairs to change into our "going away clothes." On the way up, from the landing, I threw my bouquet, aimed at Suzannah Ryan, who caught it, looking very happy. When we came down, everything we had on was brand new. Even without rice on our clothes, we were glaringly obvious honeymooners. Someone drove us to Thirtieth Street Station, where we were to board a train to New York. Waiting for it, we spotted some of the wedding guests on the platform, but we studiously ignored them and they us. We stayed at the Westbury Hotel, which a well-off New York college friend of Bill's had told him was suitable for the occasion. It seemed to us very grand. My new husband had arranged for a bottle of champagne to be in the room and a vase full of yellow roses, my favorites.

THE TROUBLE BEGAN the next morning, as we were having breakfast in our room (I in the expensive white peignoir from McKenna's in Boston that my mother had provided, Bill in silk print pajamas from his mother that he never wore again) when a bell boy knocked on the door with a telegram for me. Telegrams were serious business, and my heart jumped. It was from Bill's mother. "CALL YOUR MOTHER IMMEDIATELY," it read. "THIS IS OUR FIRST SECRET." I was alarmed. Had something happened to Mum? I dutifully called home. "Is everything okay?" "Everything is fine," she said. She sounded puzzled. "What did you call about?" Mrs. Newlin had said the telegram was our secret, so I couldn't admit to Mum that I called because my new mother-in- law told me to. "I just wanted to thank you and Dad for the wedding," I said lamely. "It was really beautiful." Later, when I asked Mrs. Newlin why she had wanted me to call my mother immediately, she just said that all mothers needed to talk to daughters after their wedding nights. It would never have occurred to me to tell my mother, or anyone else, then or later, anything at all about our wedding night; it was private.

We were to have that day in New York to rest up and then fly in the evening to Barcelona on Pan American, from what was then called Idelwild Airport. We had our passports, but since these were in our different last names, my mother had worried that once in Europe, where you had to surrender your passports when you checked in, we might not be able to share a hotel room without proof that we were legally married. (This was the case in the U.S.) She had urged us to take our signed wedding certificate with us from the church.

Not long after our slightly awkward conversation responding to the telegram, Mum called back. "You forgot the wedding certificate," she said. She was right; neither of us had given it a thought. "Mort Newlin has said he will take it up to you so that you will have it when you fly. He's going to start soon, and he should be there in a couple of hours, but he's just going to leave it at the desk and not bother you." "That's very nice of him," I said, feeling young and foolish. Bill called the Westbury front desk, told them to expect the delivery, and asked them to call us when it arrived. Then we went out and took a carriage ride in Central Park. It was around 10 in the morning.

When we came back after lunch at the Tavern on the Green, there was nothing for us at the desk, which surprised us, as it had been more than three hours since my mother's call. It took only two hours to go from Philadelphia to New York by train. After another hour, we called the desk again but were told nothing had come. So Bill called his mother. "When did Dad leave?" he asked. "He left a little before ten and he should have arrived at the Westbury a little after noon," she said. "He's not back yet, and now I'm worried about him!" It was now getting on towards four o'clock, and we were supposed to be at Idelwild, an hour away, at six. Bill went downstairs to the desk to ask in person about the delivery of an envelope. Nothing. Then his mother called. "Daddy's back," she said. "I can't tell you how relieved I am. But I don't understand where the wedding certificate is. He left it right at the front desk." "I'm glad Dad is fine," said Bill, who had not been worried in the least, knowing his father tended to get sidetracked on errands. "We'll just go without the certificate."

We finished our packing in great haste and went downstairs to check out. "Oh," said the desk clerk handing us an envelope. "A gentleman left this for you while you were out for lunch." It was, of course, the certificate. No one had any explanation for why this envelope had been so steadfastly withheld for the past three hours, and we were too young to press for an apology.

It was now five o'clock, and rush hour. The taxi driver rose enthusiastically to the challenge, weaving expertly around other cars, breaking speed limits on the freeway, but even so it was almost six when we pulled up in front of the Pan American terminal. The outside was decorated with outlines of constellations, picked out in lights. I had never seen anything more beckoning or glamorous. We raced to the counter, where there were two uniformed agents, one male, one female, in the process of shutting the gate and preparing to leave. "You're too late," said the man, without looking at a clock. "It's our *honeymoon!*" we said in chorus. The woman looked at her watch. "Two minutes. They're okay," she said to her colleague, and to us, "Run!"

There was no security line to go through, and run we did. Away from our parents and Philadelphia, to a propeller plane that would stop in Gander, Reykjavik, Shannon, and Paris before touching down in Barcelona 22 hours later. Neither of us had been to Spain before—like marriage, it was terra incognita, but we were ready to explore.

As it turned out, no European hotel had the slightest interest in that wedding certificate, ever. The first hotel clerk we offered it to found our tendering proof of marriage hilarious, and after that, we kept that paper to ourselves. We knew we were married, even if no one in Europe cared.

acknowledgments

M any thanks to the following: to the members of my writing group—Maureen Hinkle, John Malin, Gay Lord, and Bill Newlin senior—without whom, I would probably not have written these memoirs; to my daughter Eliza Carney for editing them; to my brother Bill for his fact-checking; to my son Bill for pushing them over the finish line into a book; to Domini Dragoone for her creative book design; and for the encouragement of all these as well as numerous others, especially Lucy Bell Sellers. Thanks, too, to Lucy Bell Jarka-Sellers, for her illustrations. And finally, thanks to Mariluz Vasquez, who cooked and cleaned while I wrote.

Louisa Foulke Newlin has been a teacher and educator for more than six decades. She earned a B.A. in English from Radcliffe, an M.A.T. from Johns Hopkins, and a Ph.D in Literary Studies from American University, and taught English in Washington at several high schools, public and private, and at American University; at the College of the Atlantic in Maine; at the International School in Brussels; and at the Lycée de Valbonne in France. Newlin was instrumental in the early development of the Folger Shakespeare Library's high school education programs, including the Student Shakespeare Festival, the High School Fellowship Program, and the Shakespeare's Sisters seminar. Her work has been published in many magazines and journals, beginning with a poem in *The New Yorker* when she was sixteen, and including a short story in *The Atlantic Monthly* that won second prize as an "Atlantic First." With her husband of more than 65 years, a retired Foreign Service officer, Newlin has lived in Paris, Guatemala, Brussels, and Nice, always returning to their home in the Cleveland Park neighborhood of Washington, D.C.

Printed in the USA
CPSIA information can be obtained
at www.ICGtesting.com
JSHW022321140824
68134JS00019B/1222